Dragons, Little People, Fairies, Trolls and Elves

HACHETTE Illustrated

To Claude Seignolle and Pierre Dubois
whose works and friendship have been precious allies in my explorations of fabulous kingdoms.

Edouard Brasey

Dragons, Little People, Fairies, Trolls and Elves

CONTENTS

Introduction

Month of may, month of faeries

A Midsummer Night's Dream

Halloween

Christmas and the Night of Miracles

Wunder
Garten

Introduction

The doors to Faerie and the enchanted calendar

"Unwise the man who refuses to give credence to those
fabulous creatures of this world that are faeries."
Mélusine, Jean d'Arras (c. 1500).

There are several entrances to the fabulous world of Faerie, each with its own advantages but also its dangers. For it is not without risk that one crosses the invisible frontiers separating our world from the realms of magic.

The first and plainly the simplest way is to slip between the illustrated pages of a good book of tales. But beware! Make sure you know the origins of the book. Some ancient books of magic spells have such powerfully bewitching images that the reader may well fall victim to their seductive charms, transfixed by the beguiling smile of a faery or water sprite.

Another way is to become a confirmed dreamer or daydreamer. Dreamers are inveterate explorers of the faerie kingdom, traveling with no need of transport or maps. But some dreams are said to be so powerful and seem so real that the sleeper cannot awaken, being forever ensnared by the delightful illusion into which he or she was plunged by sleep.

Contact with nature, preferably wild and unspoiled by man, is another excellent route to the realms of fancy. We have known since the days of Paracelsus and the 16th-century alchemists that faery creatures are formed from the subtlest ingredients of the four elements that constitute the universe. For that reason, they are also known as "elementals." Faeries and goblins, the most diaphanous of all the faery creatures, exist in air, clouds and wind. Mermaids and water sprites, nixies and naiads, are the denizens of the watery universe — seas, oceans, rivers, torrents, springs and fountains. The Little People, dwarfs and gnomes and other hard, mineral spirits are at home in the bottom earth and beneath the roots of trees. Spirits of fire, the salamanders, basilisks and dragons, all dwell in fire and flames.

People on solitary walks have sometimes heard the song of the elves in the wind that whistles through the trees, or may come upon a water sprite bathing in a foaming waterfall, or see the grimacing face of a dwarf imprinted on a rock, or even feel the fiery breath of a salamander as it warms its hands by a wood fire.

But these elemental creatures do not always mean well and should always be approached with extreme caution. In Devon, in the west of England, for instance, people who venture alone into forests that are inhabited by elves are deliberately led astray by the pixies. To find their way again, they must simply turn their coats inside out, put the right shoe on the left foot and hop forward 13 times. But not everyone knows that. Nixies and White Ladies that haunt the edges of ponds lure young men with their seductive looks and exquisite chanting, then force them to dive to the very bottom of the still water, where they are drowned. The most enchanting faery may suddenly turn into a grimacing witch, due to some abuse of the faery code of etiquette or the elfin code of honor — of which, it has to be said, most of us mortals have not the faintest notion.

Other enchanted doors that lead to the kingdom of magic must remain secret, because the Little People prefer to keep well away from humans who are sadly notorious for their obsessive curiosity and arrogant designs. As a protection against faery mischief, the wee folk are known by a variety of names such as "Good Neighbors," "Gentry," "Faery Godmothers," "Fair Folk" or "Themselves." The lands inhabited by elves and faeries count as the sixth continent of the world, but very few humans have ever ventured there and even fewer have returned.

So we will give no precise directions to the Enchanted Isles, the Happy Isles, the Fortunate Isles and those other islands of Faerie which according to early medieval writings may be precisely located on a map of the oceans. We prefer to keep our vow of silence concerning the whereabouts of the mythical lands of the Emerald Isle: Tir Nan Og, "Land of the Young"; Tirfo Thuinn, "Land Beneath the Waves"; Tir Nam Beo, "Land of the Living"; Tirn Aill, "The Other World"; Mag Mor, "The Great Plain"; Mag Mell, "The Pleasant Plain"; Tir Tairngire, "Plain of Happiness." There is not a sailor alive today who knows the way to these legendary isles, which are sometimes visible and sometimes submerged. The Welsh believed that faeries lived on a mysterious island in the Irish Sea, off the coast of Pembrokeshire, a place from which those sailors who were bold enough to go have never returned. The faeries who lived on this island did sometimes go to the markets of Laugharne and Milford Haven. For the English meanwhile, the kingdom of magic was centered on the Isle of Man.

Of all these isles, the most fascinating is the mythical isle of Avalon where faery ladies and their lovers feed off golden apples of eternal youth. It is here that King Arthur, mortally wounded in battle, was ferried in an enchanted craft drawn by four white swans. Once there, he was cared for by the Faery Queen Morgana, Sovereign of Avalon and grand priestess of that Paradise that the Celts believed was the location of the kingdom of the dead. According to legend, Arthur was laid to rest on that island where he remains to this day, deep in an enchanted hillside surrounded by his bravest knights. At the appointed time, he will wake from his slumbers to reign once more over the isle of Brittany.

Talking of time, and before we venture further into the invisible kingdoms, it must be understood that the passing of time in Faerie is not subject to the pitiless and artificial constraints of time in our human world. It is indeed time of an entirely different nature.

To judge by the testimonies of countless eminent elficologists and learned explorers of magical realms, faery time is governed by rules that to us appear quite arbitrary. A single minute in Faerie can last an hour, a year or even a century in mortal time. Or a year can pass in the blink of an eye. Sometimes time can run backwards or swing inexplicably between past and future. It is even said that notions of past, present and future are meaningless to the Little People who can jump from one time zone to another whenever it suits them, as effortlessly as if they were exploring the rooms of a house.

Subject to these reservations and preliminary cautions, we can now venture in all conscience into that other space and time which rules the world of fantasy. Armed with the right keys and the appropriate magic formulae, we can pass through the enchanted doors that lead to the Kingdom of Faeries, keeping to the precise dates and times of the faery calendar. For although faeries and other Little People can appear at whim, certain times of the day are better than others. Twilight, midnight or the hour just before dawn are particularly favorable. Some faeries however only appear in the interval between two blinks of an eye, which is why children were told not to keep their eyes open for too long without blinking. They might see faeries and follow them unsuspectingly to the Land of Faerie or, failing that, be left stunned and simple-minded for the rest of their days. The three nights of the full moon are also ideal times to meet faeries, but beware of encounters with witches too. Friday, the faery Sunday, is another good day. The Christian Sunday or Lord's Day is taboo in the faery world.

It is the duty of every elficologist of whatever experience to know and keep to the times and places appointed by faeries for meetings. Fail in this and you may never sleep in your bed again. The good faeries you meet in May are not the same as the witches that you encounter on Halloween. The will-o'-the-wisps that dance in the fields on Midsummer's Day are only distant cousins of the tomtes and nisses of the Great North who at the winter solstice set off in search of the new fire and help Santa Claus to distribute his presents. Water sprites found in rivers and springs do not share the murderous tendencies of still-water nixies. The mischievous elves that hide your keys in a bag of flour are not to be confused with the terrible red caps that dip their red bonnets into their victims' blood to revive the color. Every hour, every season and every place corresponds to a particular universe, populated by particular creatures with a particular way of life, habits and customs.

Let us now discover what they are.

"Did you see the road to Fairyland
I'll tell, it's easy, quite
Wait till a yellow moon gets up
O'er purple seas by night,
And gilds a shining pathway
That is sparkling diamond bright
Then, if no evil power be nigh
To thwart you, out of spite,
And if you know the very words
To cast a spell of might,
You get upon a thistledown,
And if the breeze is right,
You sail away to Fairyland
Along this track of light."

The Road to Fairyland, Ernest Thompson Seton (1860-1946).

THE GOOD LADIES
OF NATURE

In the spring, good faeries emerge from their long winter sleep to witness the buds opening and to share in the reawakening of Nature. This is one of the best times to surprise them at play and no self-respecting elficologist would dream of missing such a charming rendezvous between the winged ladies and their human friends.
But it is as well to be familiar with their customs, habits and ways of life if you are to make the most of the opportunity while avoiding the traps that these marvelous but capricious creatures set for those who allow their curiosity to get the better of them.

THE SPRING EQUINOX

"Fairies, arouse
Mix with your song
Harplet and pipe,
Thrilling and clear,
Swarm on the bows!
Chant in a throng!
Morning is ripe,
Waiting to hear.
A Wood in Faeryland, William Allingham
(1824-1889).

Faeries first appear at the time of the spring equinox when night and day are perfectly balanced. It was at this time of year that the Ancients used to bring offerings to the Good Ladies and Divinities of Nature. It was customary to paint eggs in bright colors and inscribe them with wishes before burying them in places where the faeries would find them and make the wishes come true. That tradition survives today in the Christian custom of the egg hunt on Easter morning that is such a favorite with children. The Easter egg like the spring equinox that comes shortly before Easter (just as the winter solstice comes shortly before Christmas) is a symbol of rebirth, fecundity and eternity. It marks the fruit of the union between heaven and earth and carries within it the seeds of revival.
We have it on good authority that the spring faery hibernates in a cozy nest that she builds in the hollows of trees, on hawthorn branches or sometimes in a squirrel's larder hoard. She insulates her nest with moss and down, makes a comfortable bed of rose petals, drinks a few drops of acacia nectar and spends the winter sleeping and dreaming. With the return of fine weather, she awakens as fresh as a daisy, none the worse for her long months of sleep. This explains why spring faeries are strangers to snow and cold weather that they regard as pure fabrication dreamed up by austere winter witches.

The Feast of Beltaine

"In May, the faeries have much to do."
La Teinture des physiciens et des sophistes, Gabriel d'Hervillier.

On the first day of May (Walpurgis Night), faeries move house to another hillside, preferably settling in the branches of a lime tree or by a stream where they while away the time intoxicated with dew or chasing maybugs. At night they dance on moonbeams or perform balancing feats on threads of gossamer. This is also when the child faeries are born, entering the world in the calyxes of half-opened flowers, their sweet little faces gradually unfurling in the reborn sun.

In ancient Celtic tradition, the first day of May was also the date of the Feast of Beltaine, a grand springtime festival of worship in praise of love and fecundity that marked the end of the "dark season" and the start of the "light season." Its patron was the sun god Belenos.

In the early days of May, those seeking to win the good graces of the Little People are recommended to leave offerings of fruit and milk in fields and woods. Faeries reward such thoughtfulness by providing humans with rich and abundant harvests, fertile, productive livestock and delightful gardens fragrant with a wealth of colorful flowers.

Above
Sophie Anderson (1823-1903).
"Generous towards men, good faeries were the charming guardians of nature. It was they who smartened up springtime, shaking all evil-looking creatures out of her robes. They restored calm to troubled elements and brought peace anew to human hearts."
Les Fées, Henri Durville
(1888-1923).

Below
Faerie Queen
English School (20th century)
The Faerie Queen and her enchanted retinue make their way to the Feast of Beltaine, dedicated to love and fecundity.

Right
Faerie with Wings,
Charles Folkard (1878-1963).
"For spirits when they please
Can either Sex assume, or both
In what shape they choose
Dilated or condens't,
bright or obscure,
Can execute their
aerie purposes."
Paradise Lost, John Milton
(1608-1674).

Above
Retours des Fleurs
J. -J. Grandville (1846).
Good faeries deck the spring
flowers in their multicolored
frocks and suffuse them with
intoxicating fragrances.

Right
The Flower Ballet,
George Cruikshank (1792-1878).
"When picking daisies on grassy
slopes, people often come across
circular bands of vegetation that
are darker, more dense and half
as tall again as the surrounding
vegetation. Many are semi-cir-
cular and open, others form a
perfect circle. Diameter and
width differ in each case and
they all appear to have been
drawn with the aid of a compass.
In the autumn they flush crim-
son beneath a diadem of
Caesar's mushrooms and other
brightly colored toadstools.
Legend has it that these are rings
made by faeries who danced in a
circle by the light of the moon."
Le Temple de Satan, S. de Guaita
(19th century French poet).

FLOWER FAERIES

"His tough spear of a wild oat made,
His good sword of a grassy blade,
His buckram suit of shining laurel,
His shield of bark, emboss'd with coral."
Sylvia or The May Queen, George Darley (1795-1846).

Faeries, helped by their companions the elves are the guardian spirits of trees, flowers and all plants. It is they who breathe the fragrance into flowers, deck them out
in pretty frocks that shimmer with color and give them their graceful outline, each
species of flower taking the shape — and sometimes the face — of her faery guardian.
So we find that the Rose Bush Faery is graceful and fragrant while the Poppy Faery has
bonny red cheeks and a dress that is always crumpled. In England, the Pillywiggin, no
bigger than a bee, is particularly fond of the wild flowers that grow at the feet of oak
trees. In Quebec the Redwood Faery, nicknamed "Four Time," appears as a pretty
maid some seven inches tall draped in a diaphanous robe of redwood leaves that she
wraps around her like a grass skirt. All of these faeries possess magical powers that we
can use to our advantage, provided we do not misuse them.

The origins of faeries

The word faery derives from the Latin word *Fata*, meaning the Fates. In Roman times the *Fata* were goddesses of Destiny who presided over the good and bad fortunes of men. The same word *Fata* now means faeries in modern day Italian while in the south of France (Provence and the Languedoc) it evolved to *fada* or *fade*. In the south of France today, a person who is *fada* is a simple-minded soul who has spent too long gazing at the faeries. The Scots meanwhile use the word fey to describe a person who is fated to die.

In Greco-Roman antiquity the faeries were confused with the nymphs who were named after their usual abodes. The dryads lived exclusively in oak trees while the hamadryads haunted other forms of tree. The nymphs dwelt in valleys while the preads hid away inside mountains and caves. The ancient Greeks and Romans regarded the faeries as sylvan divinities and built rustic shrines to them, covered in auspicious inscriptions.

Faeries are also good resident spirits. This explains why the word faery is often linked to sites and places where the Good Ladies are supposed to exist in folklore. Hence the countless "faery grottos," "faery ovens," and "faery holes" found all around the countryside. Mounds, tumuli, megaliths and raised stones are other signs of the presence of the Little People. In southeastern France, the "faery rock" at the spa at La Bourboule in the Puy-de-Dôme is believed to house the Mineral Water Faery. Further north, the "Midnight Stone" in Blois between Pont-Leroy and Thenay is said to spin on Christmas day. Another spinning stone in nearby Tours is said to have been placed there by faeries who carried it on their fingertips.

Primroses, the first flowers of spring, are believed to reveal the hidden treasures that are guarded by the faeries. People in Ireland plant profusions of primroses outside their front doors to ward off evil spirits. A bouquet of primroses may however be a sign of bad luck if it contains fewer than 13 flowers, in which case the number must immediately be made up with violets.

A legend from Somerset in southwestern England tells the story of a young girl who set off to pick primroses and lost her way in the forest. But when she added the thirteenth flower to her posy, a multitude of little yellow faeries suddenly appeared, showing her the way home and showering her with fine gifts. Safely home again, she told everyone about her fabulous adventure and unwittingly inspired an envious neighbor to try his luck with the faeries. Once in the forest, he picked the wrong number of primroses and was never seen again.

Again in Somerset, there is a saying that if you pick hyacinths in the woods you will remain the faeries' prisoner until someone comes to find you. It is also said that periwinkles are "witches violets" and that foxgloves are "faery gloves" that should never be picked without good reason. In Ireland, the juice of ten foxgloves is used to treat children possessed by evil spirits.

.

Left
Fairies Midst Sweet Peas, 1920, Margaret Tarrant (1888-1959). Elves are the finest musicians in the world but the melodies they coax from their enchanted instruments are so poignant that those who hear them are filled with a nostalgia that holds them in thrall forever.

Below
Bleuet et Coquelicot J.-J. Grandville, 1846, in *Les Fleurs Animées*

TREES PROTECTED BY FAERIES

Some plants belong exclusively to faeries and should not be touched by humans under any circumstances. They include the hawthorn tree, groundsel and ryegrass in which faeries make their nests. Trees are also faerie residences and should be treated with respect. In Franche-Comté in central France for instance, a beech tree is known as a *fau*, meaning faery. In Sweden it is the ash and the lime tree that are regarded as faery trees. In the shade of the sacred ash tree called Yggdrasil that was planted alongside the fountain Urd, Nordic mythology has it that the Norns wove the destiny of men. In Somerset in England, the ash and the sorb tree have the power to protect herds of livestock from attacks by witches.

The alder also enjoys the constant protection of the Little People. Story has it that an English peasant who was preparing to fell one of these trees suddenly saw his farm ablaze in the distance. Dropping his murderous axe, he ran home only to find not the slightest sign of fire. But on returning to the alder, he saw the same vision again and ran back home where the fire vanished as if by magic. Now convinced that he was the victim of an illusion contrived by the faeries, the peasant decided to proceed with his task and ignore any further distractions. When he returned home, his farm had been reduced to cinders.

The list of trees protected by faeries would not be complete without the thorny plum tree, the oak and the elder which are not really trees at all but witches in disguise — witness how they bleed when you cut a notch in the bark.

Below
Ariel, c. 1860,
John Anster Fitzgerald
(1832-1906).

Right
Ariel, c. 1915,
Maud Tindal Atkinson
(1906-1937).
William Shakespeare's play *The Tempest* is the story of Ariel, spirit of the air, who falls under the spell of the witch Sycorax. Ariel was punished for not completing certain impossible tasks and imprisoned in the bark of a pine tree for 12 years.

Faerie habitats

"There are four types of habitat, each corresponding to the four elements: water, air, earth and fire. The denizens of water are the nymphs, those of the air are the sylphs, those of the earth are the pygmies and those of fire are the salamanders. Not that these names in any way suit them. Indeed they were chosen by people who had no real understanding of faeries. I use them here purely for descriptive purposes and because they serve to invoke the creatures concerned. Nevertheless, the denizens of water are also called water sprites, those of the air are also called sylvans, those of the earth are also called gnomes, and those of fire are more commonly called vulcans than salamanders. Be aware also that water creatures have nothing to do with mountain creatures and that they in turn have nothing to do with water creatures. The same applies to sylvans and salamanders: each keeps to its own particular abode but they appear to men, as mentioned earlier, so that we may see and recognize the greatness of the Lord's creation Who leaves no element at rest and empty but worketh therein great wonders."

Paracelsus (1493-1541)

Faery migrations

"With this field-dew consecrate, every fairy takes his gait."
A Midsummer Night's Dream, William Shakespeare
(1564-1616).

Flower faeries are beautiful but fragile creatures. They are particularly vulnerable to cold weather and vanish at the first sign of white frost. According to some elficologists, faeries take advantage of bird migrations to fly away to warmer climes where they are greeted by their relatives, the djinn. It is believed that for long-distance journeys, faeries travel in tiny straw baskets attached to the wings of swallows. Indeed, one such enchanted basket was discovered just a few years ago in an English garden. But other experts insist that these baskets are quite unsuitable for long-distance travel and are only used for faery tournaments and other sporting contests.

The faerie kitchen

"Faeries do their washing in a soap bubble and cook
their soup over a will-o'-the-wisp."
Béatrix Beck (contemporary, born 1914)

What is faery food? Faery food is not the same as human food. The Reverend Robert Kirk (1641-1692), pastor of the Old Kirk, Aberfoyle, in western Scotland, remarked that the bodies of faeries were "... so spungious, thin and desecat, that they are fed only by sucking into some fine spiritous Liquors, that pierce like pure Air and Oyl; others feed more gross on the Foyson or substance of Corns and Liquors, or Corne itself that grows on the Surface of the Earth, which these Fairies steal away, partly invisible, partly preying on the Grain, as do Crowes and Mice; wherefore in this same age, they are sometimes heard to bake Bread." He adds: "Wherefore in this same age [that is, in the present time] they are sometimes heard to bake bread, strike hammers, and to do such like services within the little hillocks where they most haunt. Some whereof were old before the Gospel dispelled paganism, and in some Barbarous places as yet, enter houses after all are at rest then set the kitchens in order, cleansing all the vessels."

25

According to other sources, faeries are not content with the fragrance of foods and the vital essences of plants. They also have a taste for human foods and are particularly fond of cow's milk, butter, honey and saffron. As wrote Lady Wilde in her *Ancient Legends of Ireland* (1899), the Little People "love milk and honey, and sip the nectar from the cups of the flowers which is their fairy wine." The 12th-century Welsh author Giraldus Cambrensis meanwhile explained that faery creatures "ate neither flesh nor fish but lived on a milk diet, made up into messes with saffron."

A PENCHANT FOR MILK

Faeries are so fond of milk that they can drink an entire herd dry without quenching their thirst. Indeed farmers used to reward faeries and elves — or try and win their good graces — by leaving a small glass of milk by the hearth. The invisible creatures would lap up the precious beverage to the very last drop. This pronounced taste for milk is due to their fragile, ethereal nature, the Little People being cruelly short of that vital energy that characterizes humans. To make up for an inherent weakness that threatens their long-term survival, the Little People build up their strength at calving time, taking advantage of their invisibility to hang off the cow's udders and drink their fill with impunity.

The best authors also refer to the existence of greedy faeries known as Portunes in English and Neptunes in French who break into houses at night when everyone is asleep to do their cooking in the embers of the hearth. They also taste the remains of the dishes prepared by the mistress of the house.

It was the custom among ancient Bretons, when women had just given birth, to hold a banquet beneath an oak tree near their homes so as to attract the faery godmothers. The good ladies would arrive as fast as their wings could carry them and feast off the dishes that had been prepared in their honor. When they had eaten their fill, they would reward their hosts by bending over the cradle and bestowing the newborn babe with blessings and grace.

Mortal Midwives and Changelings

Faery children, as we have seen, come into the world in the first days of May. Young flower faeries survive on no more than dewdrops but changelings and more boisterous youngsters need something more substantial. This is why faery mothers have acquired the nasty habit of spiriting away mortal midwives to the Land of Faerie to care for their faery offspring. Occasionally they may spirit away a human baby and leave a faery baby called a "changeling" in its place.

To ward off faery kidnappers, mothers in days gone by would place magical talismans around the baby's cradle. A pair of open scissors would be left at the head of the cradle, the father's shoes were laid across the baby's quilt and strings of garlic or ash were hung from the bedroom walls. Because the faeries nearly always took boy babies, mothers would protect their sons by dressing them up as girls and calling them by girls' nicknames. But these clumsy attempts at subterfuge were never enough to deceive the faeries who would regularly raid human cradles, replacing the rosy-cheeked babe with a hairy, sickly changeling. One way to get rid of it and recover the real human baby was to force the wizened changeling to speak and admit its

Above
Decoration from *A Midsummer Night's Dream*, Illustration by Arthur Rackham.

Opposite
Life of St. Etienne, Martino di Bartolomeo (Sienna, 1389-1434).

age. Child faeries, unlike human children, are hundreds and even thousands of years old when they come into the world and for some mysterious reason, simply admitting their age forces them to return immediately to their world and return the stolen child.

Experience has shown that torture and threats are useless with changelings, and the only thing that works is to take them by surprise. One good trick is to surround the cradle with pots on the boil in the hope that when the creature awakes it will be startled into shrieking: "I am more than a hundred years old/I have seen the acorn before the oak/I have seen the egg before the hen/But I have never seen so many little pots on the boil!" If you use empty eggshell halves instead of pots, the changeling will very likely exclaim: "I have seen the egg before the hen. I have seen the first acorn before the oak. But I have never seen brewing in an eggshell before!"

When as sometimes happens these tricks do not work and the infant fails to reappear, then the human baby will remain a prisoner in the world of faeries for at least seven years. But whilst there, it will receive a first-rate education in magic and will return to the world of men as a multi-talented and gifted artist, most especially in the fields of poetry and music.

Above
Poulpiquet, voleur d'enfant, 1846, from *La Mariée de Moustoirac* by Pitre-Chevalier (Pierre Michel François, 1812-1864).
"One injury of a very serious nature was supposed to be constantly practised by the fairies against "the human mortals," that of carrying off their children and breeding them as beings of their race. Unchristened infants were chiefly exposed to this calamity; but adults were also liable to be abstracted from earthly commerce."
Walter Scott, (1771-1832).

The faery ring

"In th' olde dayes of the kyng arthour,
Of which that britons speken greet honour,
Al was this land fulfild of fayerye.
The elf-queene, with hir joly compaignye,
Daunced ful ofte in many a grene mede."
Wife of Bath's Tale, Geoffrey Chaucer (c. 1340-1400).

Standing stones, menhirs, dolmens, cairns and cromlechs are said to attract faeries who dance around them on spring nights. In northern Europe, these sacred stones are at the center of a dance known as the "Dance of the Elves." In the course of the dance the faeries pass around a precious chalice containing a magic potion, a single sip of which has the power to turn a drooling idiot into a genius. But these faeries hate to be observed at their gambols and vanish as if by enchantment as soon as an intruder disturbs their gathering.

In May one often comes across perfect rings in the middle of clearings. Elficologists confirm that these are indeed the "faery circles" or "faery rings" left by the creatures' tiny footprints as they danced the roundel all night long, hand in hand. Sometimes these rings are formed by the toadstools grown by the faeries so that they would have somewhere to rest while dancing.

Previous double page
What mysterious world lies deep in the heart of the forest?

Opposite
Illustration by Florence Harrison,1912, for *Elfin Song.*
"Those brilliant green rings we call "Fairy Rounds" that appear on lawns are the work of faeries. Even these days, when a Danish farmer discovers a new ring at dawn, he will say that faeries have been dancing there all night."
Leroux de Lincy.

Right
Come, now a Roundel,
Arthur Rackham.
In certain grass fields, mushrooms growing in a circle might be seen of a morning, and the old folks pointing to the mushrooms would say to the children, "Oh, the piskies have been dancing there last night." '
The Fairy Faith in Celtic Countries ,
W. Y. Evans Wentz (1911).

Entering the Kingdom of Faerie

*"It was between the night and day,
When the Fairy King has power;
That I sunk down in a sinful fray
And 'twixt life and death was snatch'd away
To the joyless Elfin bower."*
The Lady of the Lake, Walter Scott.

Below
*The Altar Cup in Aagerup :
The Moment of Departure,*
Richard Doyle.

Right
The Festival of the Elves,
Arthur Rackham.
In the Kingdom of Faerie
beneath the enchanted hills, faeries,
elves and goblins hold banquets laden
with an infinity of sweet meats and
exquisite magic liqueurs. But woe
betide the mortal who dares to partake
of these delicacies. At the first
taste, he will be taken prisoner
for ever.

Faery circles are privileged places where mortals can meet the good ladies, watch their frantic dancing and occasionally even dance with them. But beware, faeries do not easily let go the hand of those unwise enough to join in their games. A few years ago in Switzerland in the canton of Vaud, I met an ancient bookseller with a passionate interest in all things Faerie who had once entered one of these magical circles. He had immediately felt himself irresistibly caught up in a hectic saraband from which he only escaped on the verge of exhaustion. It is said that a companion must stand outside the faery circle and reach in to extract the hapless victim from the frantic dancing. If not, the unrepentant dancer may well be doomed to whirl around for hours or even days or months until he finally drops dead.

THE ENCHANTED HILLS OF THE ELVES

"It is night when the elves go out,
Their tunics damp and humid,
To lay beneath the lily pads,
Their dancer died from fatigue."
Théophile Gauthier (1811-1872).

Preceding double page
A Dance Around the Moon,
Charles Altamont Doyle
(1832-1893).

Below
Merlin l'enchanteur,
illustration by Félix
Lorioux (1872-1964)
for *Quand les fées*
vivaient in France (1923).

Right
Arthur Rackham,
illustration for *A Midsummer*
Night's Dream. *"... And one of*
the Faeries had received the order
to transport him to my coppice in
my enchanted kingdom."

Those who step into faery circles out of curiosity or carelessness are indeed robbed of all sense of human time. They suddenly find themselves captive in a time beyond time, Faerie time, that answers only to the most subjective of rules.

But for genuine explorers of the realms of Faerie, such incursions into magic circles offer an opportunity to visit the elvish court. They may also try circling a faery mound nine times on a night of the full moon. If they are considered worthy enough, a doorway will open in the ground giving access to the faery ballroom. But beware! The slightest sound is enough to dispel the enchantment, turning the faery palace into a dark, desolate cave.

Our explorer could also spend the night on one of these enchanted hillsides, where he or she will dream of the elvish kingdom and all its marvels. But the sleeper is almost certain to be carried off beyond dream to those imaginary countries where people are known to stay or be forced to stay forever. Remember what happened to Rip Van Winkle in the tale by Washington Irving: he thought he had been asleep for barely a few hours when he had actually spent 20 years in the realm of Faerie. When he awoke, his dog had disappeared and his gun was covered in rust.

Those who return from the Land of Faerie may indeed have a shock in store. Many a mortal carried off to Faerie Land, whether willingly or not, finds that what seemed like weeks of perfect bliss in that other world did in fact equate to centuries in mortal time. The dreamer returns to reality only to find that family and friends died long ago and that he is all alone in the world.

Our misguided adventurer into Faerie Land is doomed to spend the rest of his days filled with longing for the land of his dreams — like Thomas the Rhymer perhaps in the ancient Scottish ballad (see page 43) who was invited by the queen of Elfland to spend seven years in her enchanted kingdom.

The Ballad of Thomas the Rhymer (17th century, anon)

True Thomas lay on Huntly bank;
A ferly he spied wi' his ee;
And there he saw a lady bright
Come riding down by the Eildon Tree.

Her shirt was o' the grass-green silk,
Her mantle o' the velvet fine;
At ilka tett of her horse's mane
Hung fifty sil'er bells and nine.

True Thomas he pulled off his cap
And louted low down to his knee:
All hail, thou mighty Queen of Heaven!
For thy peer on earth I never did see.

O no, O no, Thomas, she said,
That name does not belang to me;
I am but the Queen of fair Elfland,
That am hither come to visit thee.

Harp and carp, Thomas, she said,
Harp and carp along wi' me;
And if ye dare to kiss my lips,
Sure of your body I will be.

Betide me weal, betide me woe,
That weird shall never daunten me.
Sine he has kissed her rosy lips,
All underneath the Eildon Tree.

Now ye maun go wi' me, she said,
True Thomas, ye maun go wi' me;
And ye maun serve me seven years
Through weal or woe, as may chance to be.

She mounted on her milk-white steed;
She's ta'en True Thomas up behind;
And ay whene'er her bridle rung,
The steed flew swifter than the wind.

O they rade on and further on;
The steed gaed swifter than the wind,
Until they reached a desert wide,
And living land was left behind.

Light down, light down now,
True Thomas, And lean your head upon my knee.
Abide and rest a little space,
And I will show you ferlies three.

O see ye not yon narrow road,
So thick beset with thorns and briars?
That is the path of righteousness,
Though after it but few inquires.

And see ye not that braid, braid road,
That lies across that lily leven?
That is the path of wickedness,
Though some call it the road to heaven.

And see not ye that bonny road
That winds about the ferny brae?
That is the road to fair Elfland,
Where thou and I this night maun gae.

But Thomas, ye maun hold your tongue,
Whatever ye may hear or see;
For if you speak word in Elfenland,
Ye'll ne'er get back to your ain country.

O they rade on and farther on,
And they waded through rivers aboon the knee,
And they saw neither sun nor moon,
But they heard the roaring of the sea.

It was mirk, mirk night, and there was nae
stern-light,
And they waded through red blude to the knee,
For a' the blude that's shed on earth
Rins through the springs o' that country.

Sine they came onto a garden green,
And she pulled an apple frae a tree.
Take this for thy wages, True Thomas,
It will give thee the tongue that never can lee.

My tongue is mine ain, True Thomas said;
A gudely gift ye wad gi'e to me!
I neither dought to buy nor sell
A fair or tryst where I may be.

I dought neither speak to prince or peer,
Nor ask of grace frae fair lady.
Now hold thy peace, the lady said,
For as I say, so must it be.

He has gotten a coat of the even cloth,
And a pair of shoes of velvet green;
And till seven years were gane and past,
True Thomas on earth was never seen.

The Fairy Wood, Henry Meynell Rheam (1959-1920).   43

The mysterious republic of the elves

"Their houses (that is, the Faeries') are called large and fair, and, unless at some odd occasions, unperceivable by vulgar eyes, like Rachland and other Enchanted Islands; having for light continual lamps, and fires, often seen [burning] without fuel to sustain them. [...] But if any Superterranean [that is, human] be so subtle as to practice sleights [tricks] for procuring a privacy [that is, knowledge of] any of their [faery] Mysteries, such as making use of their ointments, which as Gyge's ring, makes them invisible or nimble, or casts them into a trance, or alters their shape, or makes things appear at a vast distance, and so forth, they smite them [the human concerned] without pain as [if] with a puff of wind. And thus [the fairies] bereave them of both their natural and acquired sights in the twinkling of an eye, [for] both those sights, where once they [are] come, are in the same organ and inseparable. Or they [may] strike them dumb. [...] Their apparel and speech is like that of the

people and country under which they live: so they are seen to wear plaids and variegated garments in the Highlands of Scotland and *Suanochs* (*sunach* or tartan) heretofore in Ireland. They speak but little, and that by way of whistling, clear; not rough. The very devils conjured in any country do answer in the language of that place, yet sometimes these subterraneans do speak more distinctly than at other times.

Their women are said to spin, very finely, to dye, to tissue and embroider; but whether it be as [a] manual operation of substantial refined stuffs with apt and solid instruments, or only curious cobwebs, impalpable rainbows and a fantastic imitation of the actions of more terrestrial mortals, since it transcended all the senses of the seer to discern whither, I leave to conjecture, [just] as I found it."

Secret Commonwealth, Robert Kirk, pastor of the Old Kirk, Aberfoyle, Scotalnd (1641-1692).

The tuatha de danann people

The elves of Ireland, or Daoine Sidhes, are descended from the elvish Tuatha dé Dannann, also known as the tribe of the goddess Dana. These were hyperborean people from the distant islands beyond the North Wind who lived in Ireland for many centuries until they were defeated and enslaved by the Gaëls. The Tuatha then went to ground in the mounds, tumuli and dolmens of Ireland called the *sidh*. In the course of time they built fabulous underground palaces, sometimes likened to the castle of the Holy Grail, where enchanting faeries served noble knights goblets of magical nectar. In a story by Gervais de Tilbury, Marshall of the Kingdom of Arles in France in the year 1212, a hunter who occasionally climbs to the top of a mound in the English county of Gloucester, suddenly sees a hand appear offering him a goblet of invigorating liqueur. In an Irish tale, the hand offers an apple to Conlé the Red who is immediately bewitched and obliged to follow the faery to her underground kingdom.

The megalithic monuments found throughout the Celtic countries, from Brittany in France to England, Wales, Scotland, and Ireland, are believed to be enchanted doorways to the mysterious elvish world. One of the finest examples is Stonehenge, the circle of megaliths on Salisbury Plain in southwestern England.

Left
The Triumphant March of the Elf King,
Richard Doyle.

Below
The Fairy and the Knight,
Richard Doyle.

In Celtic tradition, the Tuatha dé Danann were venerated as an elvish people of divine extraction. Their sovereign Lord, King Dagda, was reputed to possess an angelic beauty and refinement. Like all the elves, he was a gifted poet and musician with a talent for coaxing strange melodies from his enchanted harp, sometimes funny, sometimes sad, sometimes nostalgic and sometimes powerfully soporific. His magnificent palace of Brug na Boinne boasted every wonder imaginable, especially three trees that bore fruit whatever the season, a magical cauldron that was filled with an inexhaustible supply of food and an enchanted goblet that was permanently brimming with exquisite nectar. There were always parties at the palace and sometimes humans were invited.

Dagda had four sons, each the heir to a separate kingdom. One of these sons, Finvarra, king of the Tuatha dé Danann of Connacht, desired Ethna who was the most beautiful girl in Ireland and was betrothed to a young nobleman of Connacht. One day Finvarra carried Ethna off to his magnificent underground palace to make her his mistress. Ethna's betrothed knew that the kingdom of the elves would disappear forever if it were exposed to sunlight, so he immediately threatened to excavate the mound that concealed Finvarra's palace. The latter agreed to release Ethna but not before giving her an embroidered belt that turned out to have magical powers, plunging the young woman into a lethargic state from which it was impossible to rouse her. It seemed she was forever doomed to remain the prisoner of the Tuatha dé Danann. Ethna's fiancé tried to undo the belt but it had been so finely tied by faery fingers that it defied all human dexterity. So the young Lord took his sword and with a single blow severed the enchanted bond, hurling the magic belt into the fire. Ethna instantly recovered her spirits and threw herself into her lover's arms.

Ethna survived her compulsory invitation to the court of the elves and as far as we know lived happily ever after with her human husband. In most cases however, mortals who gain access to the world of the elves have such a marvelous time that they would never dream of leaving.

It is said for instance that Prince Laeghaire, son of King Crimthann, the sovereign of Connacht, went with 50 of his most faithful warriors to the palace of Fiachna, Prince of the Tuatha dé Danann who live in one of Ireland's hollow hills. The prince and his men were so well treated by the elves that they elected to stay there forever. But a year later, Laeghaire expressed a desire to go and pay final homage to the king his father and his subjects. Fiachna gave his permission but on two important conditions: if Laeghaire and his companions wished to return to the kingdom of the elves, they were neither to dismount nor to allow themselves to be touched by anyone. The Prince of Connacht agreed to these conditions and returned to see his father who the moment he recognized his long-lost son rushed forward to embrace him. But the Prince refused to be approached and disdained the offer of his father's throne. Turning his horse about, he headed straight back for the court of the elves which he never left again and where he remains to this day. For in the kingdom of the elves there is no such thing as illness or death, only happiness and joy and endless merry-making graced by the touch of an eternal spring.

Below
A la Fête des Elfes, early 20th century color print.

Right
Au pays des fées, illustration by Félix Lorioux (1923).

At the elvish court

"The employment, the benefits, the amusements of the Fairy court, resembled the aerial people themselves. Their government was always represented as monarchical. A King, more frequently a Queen of Fairies, was acknowledged; and sometimes both held their court together. Their pageants and court entertainments comprehended all that the imagination could conceive of what was, by that age, accounted gallant and splendid. At their processions they paraded more beautiful steeds than those of mere earthly parentage -- the hawks and hounds which they employed in their chase were of the first race. At their daily banquets, the board was set forth with a splendour which the proudest kings of the earth dared not aspire to; and the hall of their dancers echoed to the most exquisite music. But when viewed by the eye of a seer, the illusion vanished. The young knights and beautiful ladies showed themselves as wrinkled carles and odious hags – their wealth turned into slate-stones – their splendid plate into pieces of clay fantastically twisted – and their victuals, unsavoured by salt (prohibited to them, we are told, because an emblem of eternity) became tasteless and insipid – the stately halls were turned into miserable damp caverns – all the delights of the Elfin Elysium vanished at once."

Letters on Demonology and Witchcraft, WALTER SCOTT.

The Enchanted Tree, Richard Doyle.
*"The Kingdom of Faery is a living world that
only the childish imagination is capable of
recreating in all its extravagance."*
Que mon désir soit ta demeure,
Dominique Blondeau (contemporary, born 1942).

THE PRIMROSE FAERY

Once upon a time there were three impoverished brothers who lived in a cabin in the mountains where they scratched a living as woodcutters. It was exhausting, thankless work and the two elder brothers, hardened by years of misery and privation, envied and coveted other men's goods. Only the third and youngest brother had kept a pure heart although he was none the happier for it. One day, deep in the heart of winter, the eldest brother was returning home from the forest, his axe tucked under arm, when he noticed a magnificent yellow flower growing in the middle of the snow. It was the first primrose of the year.

The woodcutter was so taken with the flower's beauty that he picked it to wear it on his hat and continued on his way. But after a few paces, his hat seemed to grow heavier and heavier so he took it off and there, much to his surprise, was not the primrose but a bright yellow faery. She handed him a golden key and said:

"With this key you can open the hill of gold. But beware! Be sure to choose wisely and only remove its most priceless possessions ..."

Then, slipping the golden key into the brother's hand, the faery vanished into the thin, cold air. The man had not time to recover from his surprise when there before him appeared a hill made entirely of gold. At the foot of the hill was a door and in the door was a lock. Without another thought, the man put the golden key into the lock, opened the door and stepped into the fabulous hillside.

He was surrounded by a glittering display of the finest, richest treasures the world has ever known: jewelry magnificently encrusted with priceless gems, exquisite pearls and treasure chests overflowing with gold pieces. In a frenzy of greed, and ignoring the Primrose Faery's advice, the eldest brother stuffed his pockets with gold and jewels and seized the heaviest treasure chest that he could carry. But the door immediately slammed shut behind him. "Bother!" exclaimed the man. "I've left the golden key inside. But who cares? What I have here will see me through for a very long time." And instead of returning to the log cabin to share his good fortune with his brothers, the woodcutter made straight for the town at the bottom of the mountain where he proceeded to live like a king off his new-found wealth.

When he failed to return home, the two younger brothers scoured the mountainside then gave up, presuming their brother dead, and resumed their miserable existence. But with him no longer there to help them, their lives were even harder and more miserable than before.

One day towards the end of winter, the middle brother was walking in the forest when he noticed a beautiful yellow flower growing by the side of the path. "What a lovely primrose!" he said. "I'm going to pick it and wear it in my hat."

The man did so and continued on his way. But in no time at all, the hat seemed to weigh a ton on his head so he took it off and there was the Primrose Faery once again, holding out a golden key.

"With this key you can open the hill of silver. But beware! Be sure to choose wisely and only remove its most priceless possessions ..."

No sooner had the man seized the key than

the faery vanished into thin air. Before him, stood a hill of silver and at the foot of the hill was a door. He rushed over, put the key in the lock and opened the door.

He stepped into a wonder world of silver, overflowing with priceless items of every description: chests overflowing with silver pieces, exquisitely engraved necklaces, legendary swords and solid silver jewelry lovingly crafted by elvish hands. Like his brother before him, the middle brother stuffed his pockets and walked out with all he could carry. But once again, the door slammed behind him. "Bother!" exclaimed the man. "I've left the silver key inside. The faery did warn me … But who cares? What I have here will take care of my needs for a long time to come."

And the second brother also headed straight for town without a thought for his younger brother. When he reached the town he met his elder brother and the two of them spent their time thinking of ways to squander the Primrose Faery's lavish gifts.

When the middle brother also went missing, the youngest brother scoured the mountain for days and days but to no avail. The snow melted and the fields and meadows gradually turned green again. One day, the youngest brother noticed a large, beautiful yellow flower growing right in the heart of the forest. "How beautiful it is!" he thought. "I'm going to wear it on my heart."

He bent down to pick the flower, pinned it to the inside of his shirt and continued on his way. The more he walked, the lighter he felt, until a few hundred yards further up, there suddenly was the Primrose Faery holding out a key of crystal.

"With this key" she said, "you can open the hill of crystal. But above all beware! Make sure you only take with you what you believe to be its most priceless possessions …"

And with that the faery vanished. In her place stood a translucent hill of crystal at the foot of which was a door that the younger brother opened with the crystal key.

Inside he found a magnificent collection of fine crystal vases, precious objects and delicately ornate figurines. Among them was a crystal doll with such beautiful, vivacious features that the younger brother instantly fell in love with her. "How beautiful she is!" he thought. "To my eyes she is the most priceless possession here." And leaving all the rest of the treasures, he left the hill carrying just the doll and the crystal key that the Primrose Faery had given him.

Once home, he sat the doll on a chair facing his bed so that he could look at her as he fell asleep. That night, for the first time in months, he slept perfectly and had wonderful dreams.

When he awoke the next morning, his first thought was for the crystal doll but what a surprise awaited him! There in place of the lifeless doll stood a young girl of flesh and blood who smiled at him and said: "This is your reward for choosing me and listening to your heart. For gold and jewels are all perishable whereas real love may last a lifetime."

The young man and his crystal bride were married without delay and lived happily ever after. What's more, since the young man had been careful to keep the crystal key, they never wanted for anything. The two other brothers on the other hand frittered away their last remaining riches and finished up as poor as they had started. They were sent into exile and never heard of again.

But through their fault, the golden key and the silver key have been lost forever. Only the crystal key remains. That is the one you have to look for in your heart.

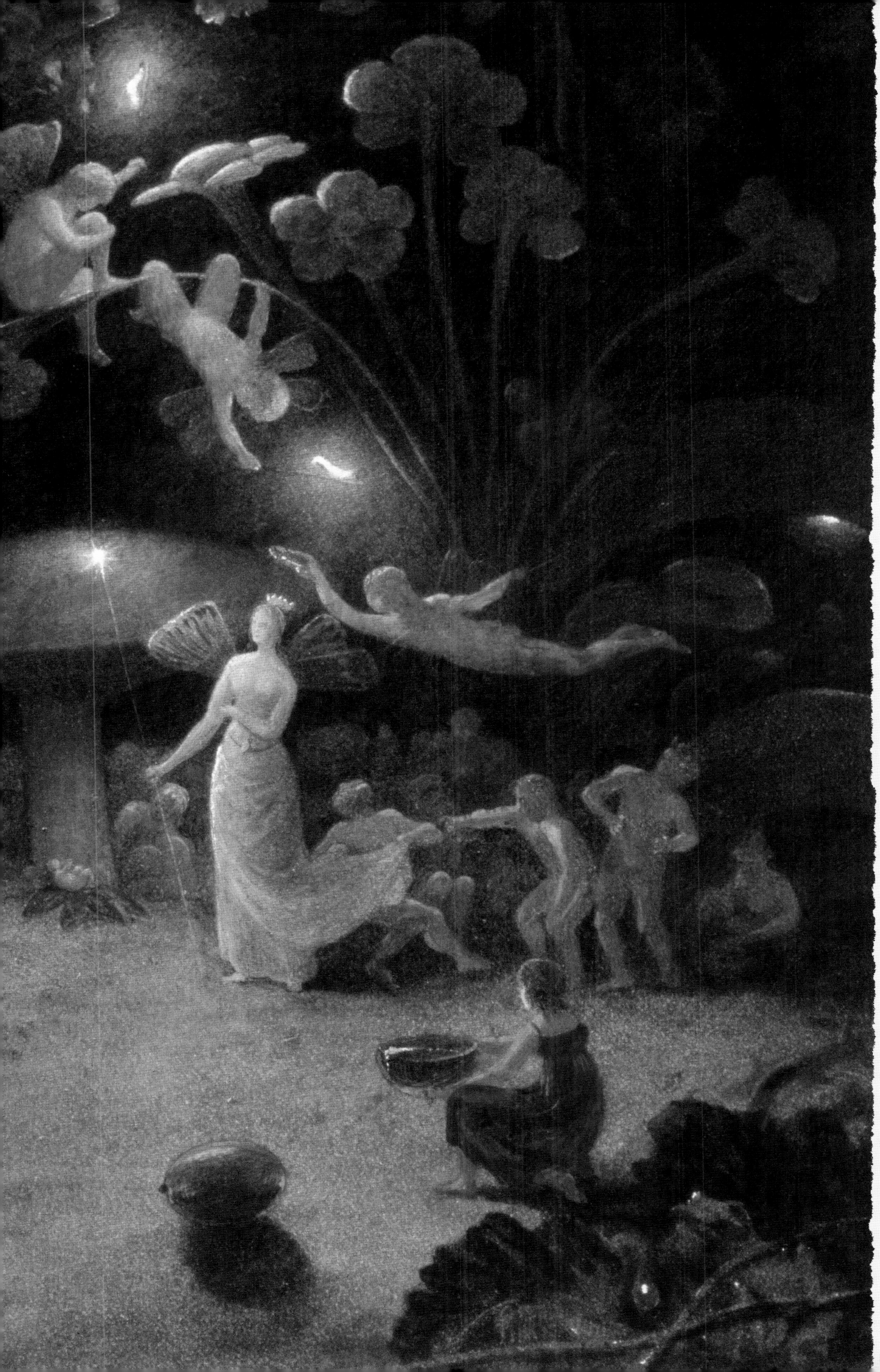

St. John's eve (midsummer night)

Sweet blossoming spring has turned to dazzling summer. Between the summer solstice and the feast of Saint John's Eve, the triumphant sun makes the most of the year's longest days to take its revenge on the shadows and cold of winter. It is a time for building huge bonfires and watching young people jump over them while making a wish that is bound to come true within the year. It is a time for singing and dancing, feast and celebration, drunkenness and folly, sensual pleasures and amorous encounters. And it is in these blissful but alas too short-lived nights of heady passion that the mortal world is said to merge with the Land of Faerie.

FAERY ENCOUNTERS

"I met a lady in the meads,
Full beautiful, a faery's child
Her hair was long,
Her foot was light
and her eyes were wild."
La Belle Dame sans Merci, John Keats
(1775-1821).

Who knows? Perhaps that young girl with the enchanting figure and bewitching look was actually a faery who had lost her way; or a water sprite recently emerged from her pond; or even a salamander fresh from the glowing embers of the bonfires on St. John's Eve? In the hot days and warm nights that mark the beginning of summer, there are countless encounters with gentle ladies and delightful young girls of such ravishing beauty that mortal men are instantly smitten and ready to follow their seductresses to the ends of the earth. But these beauties are none other than faeries

Previous double page
Scene from *A Midsummer Night's Dream*,
illustration by Francis Danby
(1793-1861).
On warm summer nights, their
Majesties Oberon and Titania,
sovereigns of the people of Faerie,
hold celebrations for their enchanted court.

Opposite
Twilight Dreams (detail),
Arthur Rackham (1867-1939).
Vaporous clouds add languorous
touches of pastel to the summer twilight: the diaphanous robes of faery
damsels on their leisurely flight
through the warm summer sky.

Right
Midsummer Eve,
E.R. Hugues (1851-1914).
"Out of this wood do not desire to go:
Thou shalt remain here, whe'r thou wilt or no.
I am a spirit of no common rate;
The summer still doth tend upon my state;
And I do love thee: therefore, go with me [...]."
A Midsummer Night's Dream,
William Shakespeare (1564-1616).

or waters sprites that carry off their human lovers to enchanted palaces where they lock them up forever.

These adorable but sometimes fatal encounters are especially common on Saint John's Eve when the air is filled with sorcery and magic. On the stroke of midnight for instance, fountains are said to flow with wine and stones turn into loaves. Stark-naked witches scour the countryside all night in search of that magical plant, St. John's Eve Grass, better known as St. John's Wort. It can be used to treat all manner of ailments, including stitches, itching and cramps or may be worn as a talisman to conjure spirits, ward off burns, black magic and demonic powers. At cock crow, the witches roll naked in the morning dew kissed by the first rays of the dawning sun. This is how they keep their complexions fresh and radiant.

At the court of Oberon and Titiana

"His belt was made of Mirtle leaves
Pleyted in small Curious theaves
Besett with Amber Cowslipp studdes
And fring'd about with daysie budds
In which his Bugle horne was hunge
Made of the Babling Echos tungue
Which sett unto his moone-burnt lippes
Hee windes, and then his fayries skipps."
Oberon's Apparell, Sir Simeon Steward.

Shakespeare's play *A Midsummer Night's Dream* is steeped in that fantastic Faerie atmosphere that characterizes the night of the summer solstice. We are introduced to the king and queen of the Faeries, Oberon and Titania, attended by their retinue. The legends that surrounded these characters were the stuff of traditional wisdom and folklore, and Shakespeare would have been familiar with all of them. Since time immemorial, the faery couple has inspired madmen and poets to cross the threshold into the invisible kingdom of the elves.

As a baby, Oberon was showered with faery blessings: beauty, harmony, joy, tolerance, artistic taste and a gift for poetry. But after a jealous witch laid a curse on him, Oberon was condemned to remain forever the size of a three-year-old child. He was forced to flee the company of men and sought refuge in the Land of Faerie

where he married Titania, the faery queen, and became the most powerful and well-loved king of the Little People. The faery couple lives in India but at night Oberon and Titania take flight to dance by the light of the moon in Nordic countries or on the eerie moorlands of the isle of Brittany. At first cock crow they hide in the buds on trees or slip into golden ears of corn, so feathery light that they make not the slightest impression on the wispy plant. In *A Midsummer Night's Dream* Shakespeare delights in evoking the domestic quarrels between Oberon and Titania and their inevitable consequences for the world of men. We learn for instance that the least dispute between the king and queen of the faeries will disturb the pattern of the seasons. Leaves turn brown in the middle of spring and it snows at the height of the hottest summer.

Queen Mab

The faery queen Titania is graced with exquisite beauty, made yet more exquisite by a subtle air of nobility. There is however according to 16th and 17th century English authors another coarser, more rustic faery queen known as Mab. In *Romeo and Juliet*, Shakespeare refers to Mab as the "faeries' midwife." She is the "Hag, when maids lie on their backs, that presses them and learns them first to bear." Some folklorists believe that Mab derived from Habundia, a witch of the medieval period who was associated with fertility rites and to whom it was customary to make offerings. But Mab might equally be a corruption of Maeve, queen of the Irish faeries, the Daoine Sidhes.

PUCK THE PRANKSTER

"I am that merry wanderer of the night,
I jest to Oberon and make him smile."
A Midsummer Night's Dream, William Shakespeare.

The faery couple, Oberon and Titania, are attended by a large retinue of courtiers among whom we find the truculent hobgoblin Puck, modeled on that best known of all the Brownies (Scottish household spirits), Robin Goodfellow. Robin was the son of Oberon and a mortal woman. When he was barely six years old he chanced to see some faeries and instantly fell into a magical sleep. When he awoke he found a document written by his father, telling him how to change his shape at will and obtain anything he wanted. These magical powers were however only to be used against wicked people in defense of their victims. Robin proceeded to play tricks on all and sundry, making fun of pretentious people, chastising criminals and goading misers, punctuating each of his tricks with peals of laughter. Finally, after a series of adventures, Robin left the world of men and was admitted to the Land of Faerie.

Previous double page
The Marriage of Oberon and Titania,
John Anster Fitzgerald.

Opposite
Will-o'-the-Wisp,
S. Barham in *Where the Rainbow Ends.*
Puck is sometimes depicted as a
will-o'-the-wisp known
as *Jack-o'-Lanthorn*

Right, top
The Captive Robin, J. A. Fitzgerald.

Right, inset
Fauns and the Fairies,
Daniel Maclise (1806-1870).
"And sometimes lurk I in a gossip's bowl,
In the very likeness of a roasted crab;
And, when she drinks against her lips I bob,
And on her withered dew-lap pour the ale."
A Midsummer Night's Dream,
William Shakespeare.

Puck is in fact closely related to the Welsh *pwca* or *pooka*, meaning a sort of truculent pixie who by day watches over herds of cattle in exchange for a small glass of milk, and by night leads lost travelers to the very edges of precipices before running away shrieking with laughter. This is why some know him as Jack-o'-Lanthorn or Will-o'-the-Wisp, rooted in the ancient figure of Ignis Fatuus, still known as Dead Candle, who personifies the restless souls of dead, unchristened children.

Robin Goodfellow

"The constant attendant upon the English Fairy court was the celebrated Puck, or Robin Goodfellow, who to the elves acted in some measure as the jester or clown of the company – (a character then to be found in the establishment of every person of quality) – or to use a more modern comparison, resembled the Pierrot of the

pantomime. His jests were of the most simple and at the same time the broadest comic character – to mislead a clown on his path homeward, to disguise himself like a stool, in order to induce an old gossip to commit the egregious mistake of sitting down on the floor when she expected to repose on a chair, were his special enjoyments. If he condescended to do some work for the sleeping family, in which he had some resemblance to the Scottish household spirit called a Brownie, the selfish Puck was far from practising this labour on the disinterested principle of the northern goblin, who, if raiment or food was left in his way and for his use, departed from the family in displeasure."

Letters on Demonology and Witchcraft,
WALTER SCOTT,

The faeries in springs and waterfalls

Hot summer days and balmy summer nights are also the times when the water faeries like to bathe in wells, waterfalls, ponds, rivers, seas and oceans. Undines and nymphs may be seen perched on the edges of wells, combing their long hair with their gold or ivory combs. Sometimes they bathe naked in the crystal ripples.

Pretty water nymphs

"A vertuous well, about whose flowry banke
The nimble-footed Fairies dance their rounds,
By the pale moon-shine, dipping oftentimes
Their stolen Children, so to make them free
From dying flesh and dull mortalitie."
The Faithful Shepherdess, John Fletcher (1579-1625).

Above
Illustration by Félix Lorioux,1923, in *Quand les fées vivaient en France.*

Below
Water Lilies and the Water Fairies, Richard Doyle.

Right
Jewels from the Deep, Arthur Rackham. The golden-haired undines possess exquisite treasures of pearl and nacre but mortals who try and steal these wonders are in danger of remaining forever imprisoned in the nymphs' magnificent underwater palaces.

The Norwegian *fossegrim* is a pretty, golden-haired water nymph barely 11 inches tall who hides in waterfalls singing sweet melodies that attract children. The Russian *roussalka* combs her blond hair while admiring her reflection in the water. The *vodianoï* have horrible green hair and bloated bodies like people who have drowned and anyone caught spying on them is instantly smitten with dropsy! Then there is the kindly nymph Sdivoneita who dwells in double-bottomed or two-tiered lakes and grants her protégés miraculous catches of fish. But be careful not to shout or swear as she will not tolerate either.

Fateful locks

"The ancient Greeks worshipped water nymphs that were called by different names depending on where they lived. Oceanids and nereids were sea nymphs, naiads, crenaeae and pegaeae were spring water nymphs, potameides were river nymphs and liimnades were lake nymphs. To these one must add the undines, fresh water faeries which according to Paracelsus, "appear in human form, dressed like us, and cannot wait to lure us with their beauty and devious ways." There were also the nixies that dwelt in still, stagnant pools and of course the mermaids, fish-maidens whose haunting melodies had the power to lure sailors to their deaths. Undines are always pretty, malicious and sometimes cruel. They wear crowns of aquatic plants and sit at the surface of the water combing their hair that may be golden or sea green. Their faces are full of laughter, with glistening lips of coral red and green eyes that sparkle in the sun. At the sight of an undine, any young man passing by will be so smitten by her beauty that he will instantly follow the nymph to her crystal palace. Once there, at the bottom of the watery depths, days seem like minutes to the young man who has no notion of Faerie time. Imagine his surprise therefore when he returns to earth to find not the people he once knew but their grandchildren. Everyone makes fun of him because of the ridiculous way he looks, dressed in clothes that went out of fashion years ago."

Elementary Spirits, KARL GRÜN

It is said that springs and wells are fed by the tears of naiads but that they dry up when the faeries are offended. In Luxembourg for instance, we find that the well at Mussy-la-Ville dries up each time a visitor draws water without believing in its magical properties, or forgets to thank the resident spirits. Spring dwellers do in fact appreciate small gifts such as garlands of flowers or rags, hunks of bread, pins, broken plates and broken bottle necks. These may seem worthless trifles to our human eyes but to the water dwellers they are priceless treasures that sparkle and glitter in the sun.

In Ireland on the first day of August, offerings were traditionally made to the spirits of the wells, and to those of the Barenton spring in the forest of Broceliande, in the very place where Merlin the Wizard once seduced the faery Viviane. Children would gather at the spring on Sundays and toss in pins and crumbs of bread. Myriad bubbles welled up from the silt and burst at the surface like crystalline fireworks, and the children would say that the spring was laughing. It was the laughter of thousands of tiny undines taking a bath in the magical waters.

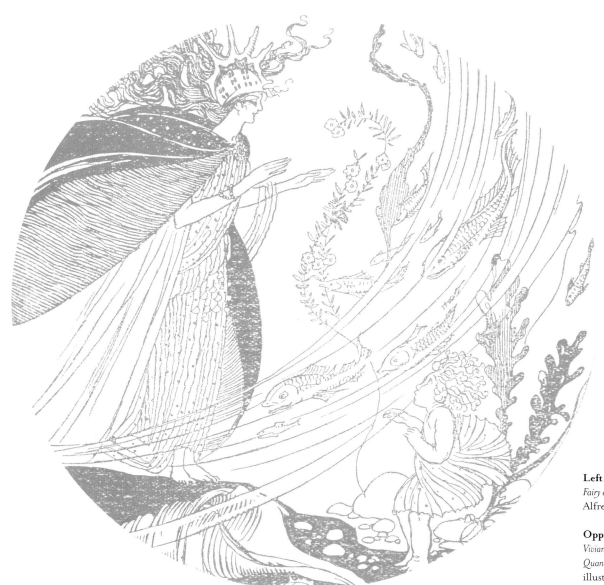

Left
Fairy and Fauns on the Seashore,
Alfred Thompson (1830-1895).

Opposite
Viviane et Lancelot in
Quand les fées vivaient en France,
illustration by Félix Lorioux, 1923.
The faery Viviane, a disciple of
Merlin the Wizard, is also the
Lady of the Lake who hides in
the watery depths and raised
the noble Lancelot as a child.

Enchanting undines

The clairvoyant theosophist Geoffrey Hodson who was a follower of Helena Blavatsky describes his undine sightings in *Fairies at Work and at Play* (1925): "The figure, which shines as if wet, is female, nude and without wings, the exquisite limbs gleam through the white auric flow, the arms are particularly long and beautiful, and she waves them gracefully in her flight. She is about four feet in height and her general coloring is silvery white, with gold stars round the head." He continues:

"She moves up the fall by a series of darting motions of exceeding swiftness, disappears from view as if into the rock, then reappears and flashes down again. As I watch her rapid movements, she appears suddenly to become languid; her form slowly dissipates and her consciousness sinks into the ground, as if to rest."

These charming water faeries delight in seducing young people who come to drink at the spring, but it is usually to lure them to a watery grave. Anyone not wishing to leave this world before their time is therefore advised to avoid isolated springs and wells and ignore the voices and languid gestures of the seductive creatures that dwell there.

Gate-crashing nixies

The Germanic nixie is a particularly dangerous type of undine with a nasty habit of gate-crashing parties at night and using her irresistible beauty to lure young men to their doom. The hapless victim finds himself caught up in a dance to the death that ends when he drowns while attempting to follow his seductress into a nearby pool. There is of course one infallible way to unmask a nixie which is to feel the hem of her dress. If it is damp, then the adorable creature before you is none other than a water spirit. But what besotted young man would ever think of doing such a thing?

These nixies are at their most dangerous on St. John's Eve when the penalty for bathing in their lakes and pools is to become their eternal slave. At the spring equinox however, nixies' tears mixed with the lake water are believed to bring beauty and eternal youth to the bathers.

Below
The Enchanted Basin, Estella Canziani (1887-1964). The surfaces of ponds and pools sometimes glimmer with the phosphorescent reflections of naiads and nixies bathing by the light of the moon.

The lovelorn Undine

In this story by Friedrich de la Motte Fouqué published in 1811, the heroine reveals her secret origins after marrying the young and handsome lord, Huldbrand de Ringstetten. "All of Nature's creations," she says, "wish to better themselves and my father, a powerful prince of Mediterranean waters, was no exception. He was determined that his daughter should possess a soul, so exposing her to many of the torments commonly afflicting mortal creatures. But we can only achieve this goal if we win the love of one of your kind. Today I have a soul and, from one soul to another, I thank you for it. My love for you is ineffable and it is to you that I shall owe that love lest you make me wretched for the rest of my days. For what is to become of me if you fear me and cast me off?"

But in truth, men are often fickle and incapable of keeping the promises that they make in a moment of passion. The handsome lord was unfaithful to his Undine, deserting her for the mortal Bertalda whose simple human love was more familiar to him than the passionate excesses of his supernatural bride. But the bonds between Huldbrand and his Undine were inalienable and failing to honor them in life was punishable by death. Undine suffocated her lover with her tears and bore him to his grave, later attending her husband's funeral in the form of a white lady. "But when we rose, the stranger in white had disappeared. Where she had knelt there was now a little spring whose limpid, crystal waters gushed over the grass then flowed on and on, gently murmuring, almost completely surrounding the knight's tomb then flowing into a tranquil pool by the side of the cemetery. For many years, the spring is said to have remained a talking point with local inhabitants. They were convinced that it was the poor, lovelorn Undine forever holding her beloved in her amorous embrace."

Enchanting Mermaids

On the shores of seas and oceans are to be found those other enchanting water creatures, the mermaids, legendary spirits with women's bodies and women's faces but a fish's tail, whose exquisite voices would lure seamen to their death.

Above
The Fisherman,
illustration by R. Kirener, 1910.

Opposite
The Little Mermaid,
illustration by Ivan Bilibine, 1937.
*"First you will come to the Sirens who enchant
all who come near them. If any one unwarily
draws in too close and hears the singing of the
Sirens, his wife and children will never welcome
him home again, for they sit in a green field
and warble him to death with the sweetness of
their song. There is a great heap of dead men's
bones lying all around, with the flesh still rot-
ting off them. Therefore pass these Sirens by,
and stop your men's ears with wax that none of
them may hear; but if you choose you can listen
yourself, for you may get the men to bind you as
you stand upright on a cross-tree mid way up
the mast, and they must lash the rope's ends
to the mast itself, that you may have the plea-
sure of listening."*
The Odyssey, Homer (translated by
Samuel Butler).

Right
The Little Mermaid,
illustration by Edmond Dulac
(1882-1953).

Seducers of seamen

The best time to observe mermaids, or sirens, are fine summer days when the sea is calm and the waves twinkle in the sunlight. It is said that mermaids are easier to see at dawn, noon or dusk, being just visible at the extreme edges of vision, far left or far right. They may be glimpsed reclining languorously on the rocks at the surface of the water, admiring their reflections in pearly mirrors whilst combing their long golden locks with ivory combs. Sometimes they wash their sheets and lay them out on the waves, the whiteness of the sheets merging with the dazzling white foam. At other times, they amuse themselves by scattering the sand with their jewels and treasures of shells, starfish, water-polished pebbles and ribbons of seaweed. Then they dive into the water laughing as tongues of blue water lick their beautiful naked breasts. But beware! Mermaids should never be gazed at directly or they will disappear in an instant, as fugitive as a mirage.

Mermaids have always caught the imagination of men. Fishermen especially regard them as givers of fabulous catches but also destructive forces whose tempestuous storms ravage fishing boats. The truth is that whereas some mermaids are good spirits most of them are malicious and should only be approached with extreme caution. The people of Lower Brittany believe that merely seeing a naked mermaid, or unwittingly brushing past one, is enough to unleash a storm. Generally speaking, the slightest physical contact with a mermaid is dangerous. The hapless mortal is doomed to follow the fish-woman to her magnificent underwater palace and remain there forever as her prisoner.

Sometimes it is one particular part of the mermaid's body that is taboo, such as her hair. In a French ballad from the Vendée area, a mermaid stranded on the sand gives the following advice to the fisherman who is about to throw her back in the sea: "Carry me in your arms and provided my hair does not touch your hand you need have no fear. But alas, should your fingers but lightly touch my locks of gold, they will remain forever attached; then I shall be forced to carry you down with me to my cave in the deep, and no power in the world shall stop me."

All seamen used to believe in mermaids — and probably still do — and some sailors even claim to have met them. Indeed, detailed descriptions of alluring sirens are very much a feature of travel stories from times past. St. Brendan, the 6th-century Irish monk who explored the Atlantic Ocean in search of paradise lost, and Christopher Columbus nine centuries later are just two of the many hundreds of seamen who claim to have sighted mermaids. Right up until the 20th century, British maritime law stated that "all mermaids found in English water" belonged to the monarch. Likewise ancient naval maps display charming pictures of mermaids in the midst of the oceans, accompanied by the words *Hic sunt sirenae* ("Here be mermaids") to emphasize the supremacy of these fabulous creatures of the seas and oceans where men once ventured in fear of their lives.

The soul of mermaids

"There is neither fish nor carp
That it has not moved to tears.
Only the mermaid
Has never stopped singing.
Sing, mermaid sing,
You have all you need to sing,
With the sea to drink,
And my lover to eat."
Song of Poitou.

A large part of that fear, it has to be said, was rooted in the belief that mermaids were creatures from hell that seduced men to devour their bodies and steal their souls. Actually it has never been proved that mermaids eat human flesh and in all likelihood the word "eat" (in the song above) was used metaphorically to suggest their lascivious appetites. The accusation that mermaids steal human souls likewise stems from a tragic misunderstanding.

It should be explained that in common with other Little People mermaids were originally conceived without the immortal soul that remains the exclusive privilege of human beings. But in His infinite mercy, the Creator granted mermaids and other faeries an infallible means of acquiring that incorruptible soul that they so cruelly lack. All they have to do is win the love of a man and become his bride. Through the sacred bond of marriage the faery creature becomes her husband's equal and worthy of receiving her own immortal soul. But victory comes at a price and sometimes the faery creature must make terrible sacrifices to win a man's love. We find this poignantly illustrated in Hans Christian Andersen's celebrated tale about a little mermaid who is forced to exchange her voice and fish's tail for a pair of human legs. But each step she takes is agony and her human lover deserts her for another. Overcome with grief, the little mermaid throws herself into the sea where she is transformed into foam. Finally, thanks to her infinite and unconditional love, she is rescued from oblivion and changed from a mermaid into a graceful sylph, spirit of the air.

The mermaid is like the sea from which she is born: serene and tranquil one moment, violent and raging the next. And like the sea, she embodies all forms of passionate love from the femme fatale who devours her lovers to the saintly figure who is ready to die for love.

Opposite
Illustration by
Hermann Hendrich (1854–1931) in
The Rhine Gold.

Right
The Lorelei,
Karl Egas (1835).

The Lorelei

I'm looking in vain for the reason
That I am so sad and distressed;
A tale known for many a season
Will not allow me to rest.

Cool is the air in the twilight
And quietly flows the Rhine;
The mountain top glows with a highlight
From the evening sun's last shine.

The fairest of maiden's reposing
So wonderously up there.
Her golden treasure disclosing;
She's combing her golden hair.

She combs it with comb of gold
And meanwhile sings a song
With melody strangely bold
And overpoweringly strong.

The boatman in his small craft
Is seized with longings, and sighs.
He sees not the rocks fore and aft;
He looks only up towards the skies.

I fear that the waves shall be flinging
Both vessel and man to their end;
That must have been what with her singing
The Lorelei did intend.

Die Lorelei, HENRICH HEINE,
(Translated from the German by David A. Grace)

The Sea Maidens,
Evelyn de Morgan (1855-1919).

Nighttime washing women

"There is no finer thread than that of the moonlight spinners.
The morning sun finds them in their dew-drenched fields
Ready to spin his mane of gold."
Ariane et les autres, Antoine de Marville.

On long summer evenings or during the hot steamy nights of the summer solstice, fleeting figures may be seen to hover over lakes, ponds and springs that dissipate by morning. They are known as maidens, white shadows, washing women or nighttime singers and they sing by the light of the moon while plunging their laundry into the stream. They beckon to passersby out late at night and ask for help wringing out the washing. But then they twist their victim's arm behind his back and drag him down with them beneath the water.

White ladies

Top
Illustration by Arthur Rackham, early 20th century.

Above
Les Lavandières de nuit, Jean-Edouard Dargent (1824-1899). Night-time washing women are sometimes known as nighttime singers or little washers of death. These ghoulish creatures thought to be the specters of infanticide mothers, are eternally doomed to wash blood-soaked linen, beating and wringing the cloth incessantly as if to further mutilate their slaughtered babes.

Unlike the cruel night-time washing woman, the white lady is usually a good spirit that helps lost travelers find their way or brings food to children and lonely shepherds lost in the woods. She visits stables holding a lighted candle and drips the hot wax onto the forelocks and manes of horses that she then plaits with the greatest of care. White ladies are regarded as resident spirits that haunt the places where they lived and died, sometimes in tragic circumstances. They are usually dressed in white and more rarely in green, red or black when they come as harbingers of misfortune, like the Lady of the Lamenting Heather of Lüneburg (the *klage Weib*) that visits humans to warn them of impending death. Ladies wearing black gloves bring ominous tidings while those wearing white gloves come with tidings of joy. Still today in Germany, there is a white lady known as Bertha that appears at the birth of crown princes to protect them with blessings. She is closely related to Holda, Queen of the Woods who bathes under the noon sun while combing her long hair, and to Ostera, to whom it was customary to offer lilies of the valley.

The Lady of Le Puy

"Often at sunset or sunrise, strands of whitish, bluish, pinkish, greenish vapor may be seen to emanate from the grotto of the Faery of the Bec Dupuy, near Dinan, in Brittany, rising and falling, thickening and then finally dissipating to reveal a woman of divine beauty. She is known locally as the Faery or Lady of Le Puy and wanders along the shores dressed in clothes that shine with all the colors of the rainbow. Sometimes she sits on the grass on the cliffs or flies as light as a bird over the grassy moorlands. She speaks to no one and flees at the sight of man. Today she languishes among the rocks, lamenting her lost powers. For once, the sound of her voice was enough to calm the raging winds and soothe the violent storm. Every morning, fishermen preparing for a day at sea would leave offerings for her on the shore and she would grant them favorable winds and plentiful catches. The women,

sisters, lovers and daughters of absent men would lay garlands of flowers at the entrance to the Lady's grotto, which was guarded by a pack of invisible barking dogs ready to devour anyone foolish enough to force an entry. But now that people have stopped worshipping idols, the Lady is seldom to be seen. Her rare appearances today bode ill, and the shore is often strewn with the bloody reminders she has left in her wake. Her last appearance was to tell a shepherdess that her lover had drowned swimming the mouth of the River Rance on his way to see her, and that she too would die. Since the clergy in Saint-Suliac exorcised the Lady from her grotto, she may occasionally be seen wandering on moonlit nights. But she flees as soon as anyone approaches and all her powers have deserted her."

Le Folklore de la mer, PAUL SEBILLOT (1843-1918).

LA FÉE

GHOSTLY APPARITIONS

White ladies are more likely to be seen in hot weather, so the best time to meet one is in summer, when they appear at certain places and at appointed times.

A white lady holding a set of keys is reported to appear daily at midday precisely in the castle of Baden. Another makes an appearance every seven years in the cellars of the castle of Walsfortsweiler where there is buried treasure. A third allows herself to be seen every year in Osterode on Easter Sunday, when she goes down to the river to bathe before disappearing among the ruins of the castle. When a member of the royal house of Parma was about to die, an old woman dressed in white would go and sit by the hearth. The ghostly specters that roamed the passageways and keeps of the royal houses of Neuhaus, Rosenherg and Hohenzollern foretold the impending death of a crown prince. At the Hohenzollern castle, the white lady would sweep the floors when death was nigh.

White ladies would also appear in the Bourbon castles in France before the death of a prince. On the eve of his execution, Louis XVI actually asked his defense lawyer Chrétien Malesherbes (who was to follow his client to the guillotine) whether he had seen a woman in white wandering the corridors. This could well have been the famous Lucie, a white lady still known to haunt the castle of Veauce in the land of the Bourbons. Every year this early 11th-century castle built on a rocky peak attracts droves of tourists who come in the hope of glimpsing Lucie at the end of the covered way. In Scotland and Ireland, the harbinger of birth and death is the banshee (or banshie), a sort of guardian spirit usually attached to a particular clan or family that lets out a blood-curdling, lugubrious shriek when the lord is about to die. The banshee perches at the top of the keep, howling for hours with such anguish and sorrow that anyone hearing it is frozen with horror.

Over the Rooftops, André Castaigne,
in *Century Magazine*, Sept. 1898.

The banshie

If I am rightly informed, the distinction of a
banshie is only allowed to families of the pure
Milesian* stock, and is never ascribed to any
descendant of the proudest Norman or boldest
Saxon who followed the banner of Earl Strongbow,
much less to adventurers of later date who have
obtained settlements in the Green Isle.
Several families of the Highlands of Scotland
anciently laid claim to the distinction of an
attendant spirit who performed the office of
the Irish banshie. Amongst them, however, the
functions of this attendant genius, whose form
and appearance differed in different cases,
were not limited to announcing the dissolution
of those whose days were numbered. The
Highlanders contrived to exact from them other
points of service, sometimes as warding off
dangers of battle; at others, as guarding and
protecting the infant heir through the dangers
of childhood; and sometimes as condescending
to interfere even in the sports of the chieftain,
and point out the fittest move to be made at
chess, or the best card to be played at any other
game. Among those spirits who have deigned
to vouch their existence by appearance of late
years is that of an ancestor of the family of
MacLean of Lochbuy. Before the death of any of
his race the phantom chief gallops along the sea
beach near to the castle, announcing the event
by cries and lamentations. The specter is said to
have rode his rounds and uttered his death cries
within these few years, in consequence of which
the family and clan, though much shocked, were
in no way surprised to hear by next accounts
that their gallant chief was dead at Lisbon,
where he served under Lord Wellington.

Letters on Demonology and Witchcraft, WALTER SCOTT.

* Milesians were the descendants of Miledh. According
to Celtic myth, Miledh came to Ireland from the East a
millennium before the birth of Christ, and is the supposed father of the Irish nation. (Translator's note)

Melusina, the Serpent Faery

Apparitions of beautiful ladies, whether water faeries or phantom faeries, are never innocent and just as likely to bode good as evil. Indeed there is a slim line between the two and it takes relatively little for joy to slide into despair. Usually it all depends on obeying to certain rules and taboos, as illustrated here in this 12th-century legend about the faery Melusina.

Melusina, meaning "marvel" was the daughter of Elinas, king of Albania, and the faery Pressina.

One day when Elinas was out hunting, he met Pressina by a spring where he had stopped to quench his thirst. He fell in love with her immediately and asked her to be his bride. The faery accepted on one condition: the king was to swear not to visit her while she was in childbed. Elinas gave his word and they were married forthwith.

A few months later, the beautiful Pressina was delivered of three ravishing daughters, Melusina, Melior and Palatina. Elinas, beside himself with joy, completely forget his promise and burst into his wife's bedchamber while she was bathing her infant daughters.

"Oh wretched man," she exclaimed. "You have broken your promise and now I must leave you forever."

And taking up her three daughters, she disappeared.

Pressina sought refuge on the Lost Isle, so called because even those who had visited it many times could only find it again by chance.

Every morning, the faery took her three daughters to the top of a mountain from where they could see Albania, the land of their birth. And each time, Pressina would weep for the kingdom from which she was forever banned and for the king whose breach of promise had ruined not only his own life but also the lives of his wife and children.

When Melusina was 15 years of age, she swore to avenge herself of this father who had been the cause of their exile. She and her two sisters left the Lost Isle and set out for their father's palace in Albania where Melusina cast a spell on Elinas imprisoning him in the forest of Brumbelio.

But the faery Pressina bitterly resented Melusina for having taking it upon herself to punish her father, and condemned her daughter to change shape each Saturday. From the waist up she would remain a beautiful woman but from the waist down she would be afflicted with a grotesque serpent's tail. And this was to happen every Saturday until Melusina found a man who would consent to marry her on

condition that he should never see his wife on that fateful day. "If there is such a man and he keeps his word, you shall soon be released from my spell and live happily ever after surrounded by numerous children. But if he breaks his word, you shall remain a serpent forever."

Melusina therefore left her mother and sisters and set out into the great wide world in search of a man who would release her from her spell. She crossed the Black Forest, then the forest of the Ardennes, eventually reaching the forest of Colombiers in the county of Poitou on the estate of Lord Raimondin, son of the Count of Forest.

One day, the Lord Raimondin was returning home from a wild boar hunt and looking for a place to quench his thirst. He stopped by a spring called the Fountain of the Pretty Thirst or Fountain of the Faeries because this was where they were wont to gather. There he saw the most beautiful woman he had ever seen, Melusina, who did as her mother had said and agreed to become Raimondin's wife on condition that he should never attempt to see her on Saturdays. But alas, should he break his word, even once, she would be forced to depart never to return and their life together would be forever ruined.

Naturally Raimondin swore to keep his word, considering it a small price to pay for the joy he would feel at having such a beautiful woman for his wife.

The marriage took place and Melusina used her magic powers to build Lusignan Castle next to the Fountain of the Pretty Thirst. The Count of Poitiers gave the newly-weds as much land as could be encircled by the skin of a stag cut into thin strips, which was a great deal of land indeed. Melusina also built castles in La Rochelle, Cloître-Malliers, Mersent and many other places. These castles would have been perfect but for a few details — a missing stone, a crooked wall, a lopsided window — that betrayed their faery origins. For faery works of art are conceived in an ideal world and cannot be revealed in their true beauty and harmony to an imperfect world such as ours. That is why, no matter how beautiful, they must always display certain imperfections when they materialize on Earth.

Likewise and for the same reasons, each of the eight sons that Melusina bore the Lord of Lusignan was marked by a physical deformity. Guy had one blue and one red eye whereas Regnault had a single, exceptionally sharp eye. Urian had one eye higher than the other while Odon had an exceptionally large ear. Antoine had a lion's claw birthmark on his cheek and Froimond had a hairy birthmark on his nose. Orrible was valiant but ugly and Geoffrey had an extra eye in the middle of his forehead and a huge tooth that protruded from his mouth like a boar's tusk.

But despite their strange and even repulsive appearance, all of Melusina's sons were courageous and noble-hearted and forged powerful alliances. Urian married the daughter of the king of Cyprus, Guy married the king of Armenia's daughter and Regnault married the king of Bohemia's daughter. Antoine wedded the Duchess Christine of Luxembourg.

The Lusignan side of the family also founded lines within the noble houses of Die, Valence, Lezay, Marais and Saint-Valérien. Their direct descendants are the Counts of Angoulême and La Rochefoucault, Saint-Gelais and Eu together with the Earls of Pembroke, in Wales. As for Melusina and the Lord Raimondin, they lived happily as man and wife for 24 years.

But one Saturday alas, Raimondin's brother Renaut arrived at Lusignan Castle and asked to see Melusina. Raimondin explained that this was not possible because on Saturdays his wife spent the day bathing, concealed from view in a tower where no one, not even her husband, was allowed to see her. But the perfidious Renaut planted doubt in his brother's mind, saying: "You allow your wife too much freedom and she shamelessly abuses your trust. How can you be sure that she is bathing alone in her tower and not entertaining her admirers who make fun of you under your very nose?"

From that day forth, Raimondin no longer slept peacefully in his bed and forced himself to leave the castle every Saturday so as to avoid the temptation to spy on his wife in her bath.

But alas, one day he could stand it no more and breaking the promise he had made 25 years earlier, he climbed to the top of the tower and with his sword, pierced a hole in the door that concealed Melusina from view. He placed his eye against the hole and shrieked when he saw the monstrous sight that awaited him.

Melusina was taking her bath while carefully combing her long silken hair. The top half of her body was perfect in every way and exactly as Raimondin had always known it. But from the waist down, in place of legs was an immense serpent's tail that splashed about in the water.

When she realized that her husband had betrayed her, Melusina wrung her hands in anguish.

"Oh wretched man!" she said. "Had you waited but one more Saturday I would have been forever released from the curse that has weighed upon me. But now it is too late my love. I must depart and you will never see me again."

And stricken with grief, she sang her last farewell:

"Adieu my heart, adieu my love,
Adieu my gracious friend,
Adieu my precious jewel,
Adieu my kind and gentle lover,
Adieu my gracious husband,
Adieu my heart's true friend ..."

And all at once, she turned into a winged serpent and flew out of the window. Ever since then, Melusina's ghost has haunted the environs of Lusignan Castle, especially on stormy nights when the castle echoes to her mournful cry as she circles the highest towers. People say she is doomed to fly like a winged serpent until Judgment Day.

As for the Lord Raimondin, he never recovered from the loss of his beloved wife. He left his castle and became a hermit in the monastery of Montserrat ("serrated mountain") in northeast Spain.

Right
Mélusine, from *Histoire de la magie*,
Emile Bayard, c. 1500.

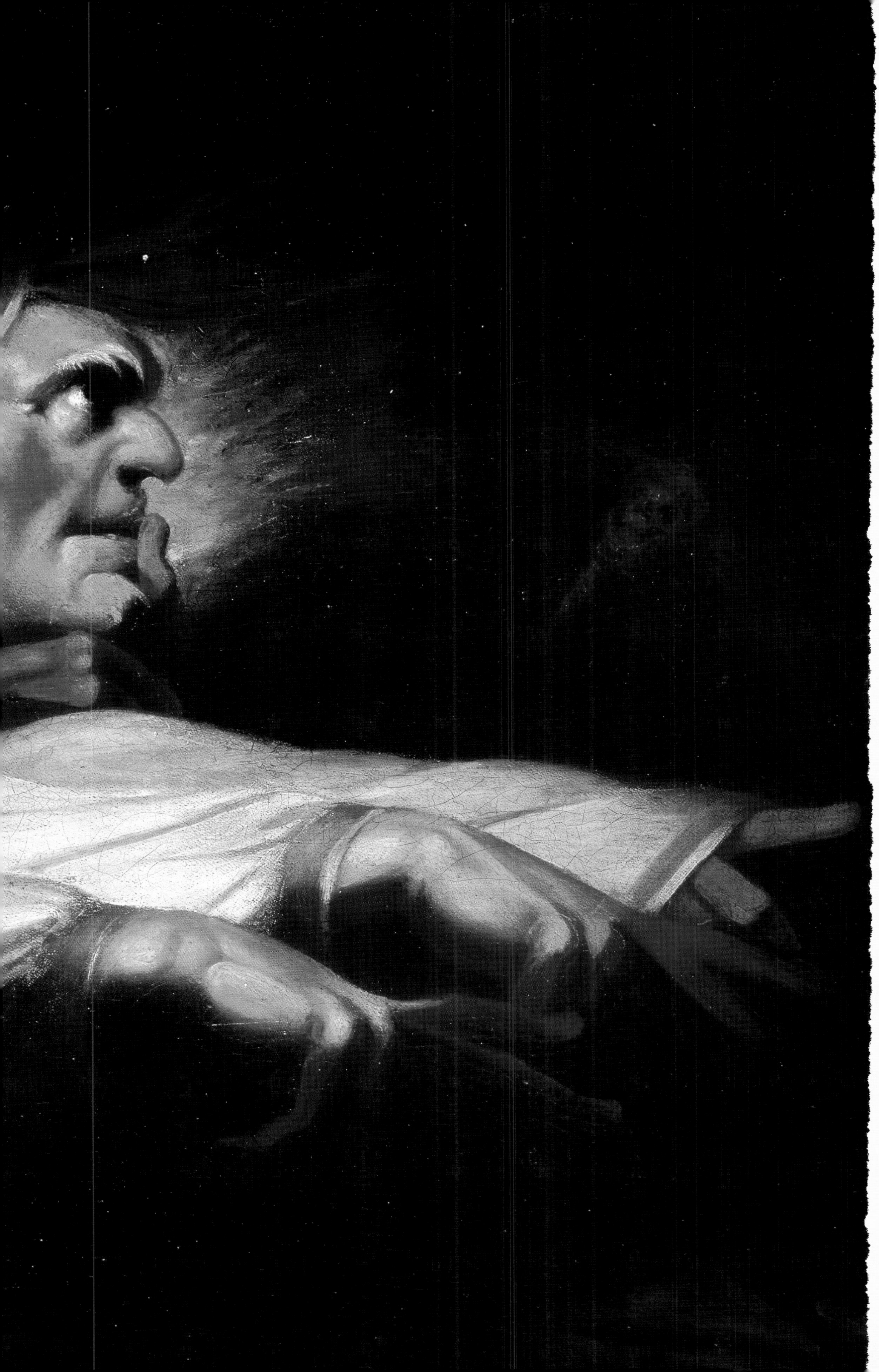

THE DARK SEASON

Fine summer days are growing shorter. The sky is heavy with black clouds and the plowed fields are lashed with rain. Autumn is upon us in shades of russet and gold when earthy colors of tree and land blend with dead leaf and vine and fragrant hues of moss and mushroom.

In the dripping woods beneath the softly falling leaves, charming flower faeries have been replaced by old and wrinkled gnomes whose gnarled faces are printed on the bark of trees and whose caps are indistinguishable from the caps of cep and boletus mushrooms. Gatherings of ravishing undines bathing naked in summer pools and rivers have made way for witches' Sabbaths and hags on broomsticks. The graceful, joyous realm of Faerie now reveals its sinister, terrifying side.

THE FEAST OF SAMHAIN

"There are only bloody faerytales.
The origins of every faerytale are steeped in blood and fear."
Franz Kafka (1883-1924).

Just as the Feast of Beltaine on the first day of May marked the beginning of the "Light Season" in the Celtic year, so Halloween, or Allhallows Eve, once the Feast of Samhain, marked the beginning of the "Dark Season" on the first day of November. This date, which corresponds to the Christian festival of All Saints, was the day the ancient Celts worshipped the dead and paid tribute to Samhain, the god of Death, who they sought to appease with offerings and sacrifices.

Preceding double page
Trois Sorcières
Henry Fuseli (1741-1825).

Below
Witches' Sabbath, c. 1821,
F. de Goya y Lucientes (1746-1828).

Opposite
Nocturnal Spires,
Edmond Dulac (1882-1953).
In about the year 735 Pope Gregory III replaced the Feast of Samhain with the Christian Festival of All Saints. It was preceded the day before by Allhallows Eve, now shortened to Halloween, a popular festival with pagan overtones that survived in Ireland, Scotland and New England before eventually spreading to Europe.

On Allhallows Eve, the Faerie kingdom flings open its doors releasing all the creatures of the night, that then become visible and mingle with humans. But unlike the Feast of Beltaine when the woods and fields are the playgrounds of delicate faeries, laughing elves and mischievous pixies, Allhallows Eve is given over to a ghoulish band of accursed creatures: evil witches, hideous demons, ghosts and the living dead, vampires and nosferatus, werewolves and the dogs of hell, snickering demons,

sulphurous incubi, succubi and nightmares. These creatures of the night are known collectively in Celtic tradition as the Host or the Unseelie Court, as opposed to the Seelie Court which is composed of the faeries and airy elves. On Allhallows Eve, humans are careful not to linger in the woods or on the edges of cemeteries lest they should suddenly be set upon by legions of evil and bloodthirsty creatures that will punch, pinch and torment them in a thousand different ways before dragging them through the gates of Hell. What makes such dangerous encounters even more frightening is that Halloween, which marks the start of the magical year, does not feature in the normal calendar. In fact, it is not a night at all but a time outside time, subject to the unpredictable, whimsical rules of Faerie cycles rather than the orthodox rules of the human calendar. As such, it is as likely to last a few hours as a few centuries, and many a mortal carried off on the last day of October by a band of witches on broomsticks has remained forever trapped in the black magic of Halloween. To ward off its evil powers, it was the custom in ancient times to light big bonfires on Halloween and hold celebrations where people would dance and sing to overcome their fear of darkness and death.

Left
Mother Goose, 1913.
Illustration by Arthur Rackham.

Above
Mother Goose, Rackham.

Opposite
Calendrier des contes de fées,
anonymous illustration, 1905.
Woe betide the foolish man who
ventures out alone on Halloween!
For the woods and moorlands are
haunted by heinous spirits that pursue and torment their hapless victims. To ward off such fateful
encounters it is recommended to
wear talismans or pendants, or use
walking sticks of ash or sorb that
have the power to repel evil spirits.

Following double page
Jack o' Lantern, 1872,
Arthur Hugues (1832-1915).

The Witches of Halloween

"On the hillside beneath the shivering moon,
Naked save for their masks of clay,
Leap young witches goaded by desire and fear."
Jean Houbert.

Beware the spells of Halloween! It is the hour when the Green Lady of Caerphilly haunts the dark passageways of ruined castles before hiding in the clambering ivy. In a river in Yorkshire, England, lurks the odious Jenny Greenteeth, a sort of greenish harpy with long hair and sharp pointed teeth that lures children down to a watery grave. There is Gwaenardel, a bloodthirsty vampire that inspired many an Irish poet. After a short, brilliant life, her acolytes also turn into vampires.

On Halloween, the cannibalistic, one-eyed Black Annis hides inside oak trees waiting to seize lost children in her long clawed fingers and devour their tender flesh, later using their skins to decorate the walls of her cave. which is known as "Black Annis' Boudoir." In Scotland a witch called Mrs Widecomb turns into an oak tree growing at the side of the road and entwines her long, thorny branches around cows' udders to suck out their milk. A witch in Yorkshire is said to have found an easier way of extracting this precious beverage: she simply "milks" the legs of the milking stool that eventually produce a warm, creamy liquid. In Russia, Poland, Bohemia and Slovakia, the *notchnitsa* (or "Witches of the Night") slip into the bedrooms of newborn babes to strangle them or bite them till they draw blood. In Bulgaria, a similar sort of hag with a calf's head leans over infants' cradles and poisons them with her pestilential breath.

Scandinavian witches also have a nasty habit of riding horseback on human beings, straddling them till dawn using magical bridles called *gand-reid* that they make out of bones and strips of skin scavenged from dead bodies. Other witches prefer to make garters of wolf pelt, renowned for its speed. Others still are transported through the air by a demon in the form of a cat, goat or griffin.

Left
Trois femmes et trois loups,
Eugène Grasset (1841-1917).

Above
A Witch representing Night,
19th-century German School.

Opposite
La Ronde de dame sorcière,
illustration by L. Bailly, ABC,
Sept. 1925.
"Observe the moment when the moon shall be in conjunction with Mercury and if it should fall on a Wednesday in spring take a strip of young wolf pelt and fashion it into two garters. Then in your own blood, mark them with the words: Abumalith cades ambulavit in fortudine sibi illius. And you will be amazed at how fast you will go with those garters around your legs."
The Book of Secrets, Albertus Magnus
(Albert von Bollstädt, 1193-1280)

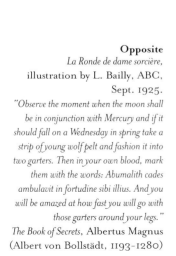

FLY BROOMSTICK, FLY!

*"And suddenly from all around in the waters, hills
and woods, issue specters, dragons, vampires, gnomes
and ghouls of fiendish imaginings;
and witches escaped from their deserted sepulchers whistle
through the air on their rods of birch [...]."*
La Ronde du sabbat, Victor Hugo (1802-1885).

Halloween is also a time for witches' Sabbaths, that diabolical gathering of wizards, witches, demons and fiends of every description that witches can only attend on a "broomstick," so-called because it must be made of broom. She places a candle on the broomstick and utters the magic words: "White stick, black stick, lead us whither thou wilt by devil!" But before flying out through the chimney on her faithful instrument, the witch usually strips naked then smears herself all over with a magical ointment that helps her to fly faster.

This appetizing concoction is made from a mixture of different plants including aconite, nightshade, belladonna, mandrake, hemlock and lily, preferably blended with the fat from dead, unbaptized children. Whether it really does possess magical powers or simply acts as a powerful hallucinatory drug we shall never know but its use is attested since the 2nd century BC if we are to believe Apuleius's account of the witch Pamphile's transformation in the *Golden Ass*. This is how he describes her metamorphosis into an owl:

"She opened a certain coffer and took out several small boxes. Removing the lid from one of these boxes, she scooped out some ointment and rubbed herself all over with it, smearing her body from the tips of her toes to the crown of her head. Then she leaned over the lamp for a long time, muttering incantations, until finally her limbs started to jerk and twitch. Gradually, as the twitching grew less violent, she sprouted little feathers and grew long wings and her nose hardened into a hooked beak. So it was that Pamphile turned into an owl."

(Translated from the Latin by Jack Lindsay)

Above and below
Under the Windows, 1978,
illustration by Kate Greenaway
(1846-1901).

Left
Anonymous illustration
in *Jugend*, 1909.

Following double page
Elfin Revellers, 1900,
Arthur Rackham.
The most favorable places to
hold witches' Sabbath are
a crossroads where four roads
meet, by a gallows, a dead tree
or at the top of a mountain.
The most notorious Sabbaths
were held on the Brocken in
the Harz range in Germany,
on Bald Mountain, near Kiev,
or on the Puy de Dôme in
the Auvergne, France.

Arthur Rackham

The Witches' Sabbath, 1515
Hans Baldung Grien. (1484-1545).

Rain witches

In the autumn, certain evil witches and wizards were said to be in charge of rainfall. The witch Ganache for instance would dip her broomstick into a pail and let it drip over the damp November landscapes. In some areas the rain is known locally as Mother Banard, a daughter of the west wind with long gray hair that she allows to trail in her soup. Sometimes she weeps until the end of January and her tears form great blobs of fat in the stock used for cabbage soup. In the Yonne region in France, people talk of a demonic washing woman with hooked fingers and big red eyes known locally as "La Beufflerie" (Old Beefy). She attracts people out walking at night to drown them in the washhouse over the Dargeot spring. In the Nivelles region, a warmly wrapped-up woman is said to wander the roads and highways in rainy weather kidnapping children who she bundles up in her cape.

In Brittany, people fear an old bogeyman called Sacrispin who makes it rain by plunging his shirt into the black, stagnant waters at the bottom of his well. In the Loire-Atlantique, the marshes of Saint-Philibert are haunted by a ghost called Louis Courtois, so shy that it throws itself into the water the moment anyone approaches. In the dark season, covered playgrounds in schools are haunted by a type of villainous gnome known as a *jacquet* that pushes children out into the rain to catch their death. Finally there are the *cra-cras*, rain elves that delight in splashing about in puddles. All of these cold, sinister spirits are part of that evil horde of damned creatures that gather on the night of Halloween.

Evil spirits

*"Through the black grass
Go the Kobolds
The mournful wind sighs deeply,
We want to believe."*
Charleroi, Paul Verlaine
(1844-1896).

Other demonic spirits make the most of Halloween to perform devious acts of sabotage that threaten the peace of mind and sometimes the life of mere mortals. In Scotland for instance the faeries gather on the moors to dance all night but the grass where they have danced withers and dies and the soil is left forever barren. Anyone setting foot on this cursed ground is sure to die in an instant unless they should happen to have a horseshoe in their pocket or a four-leafed clover sewn into the lining of their jacket. In Greece there are the dreaded *Vrykolakas*, vampires that rise from the dead at night to drink the blood of relatives who failed to give them a decent burial. In Hungary we find incubi called *Liderc* that torment weeping widows by masquerading as their deceased husbands.

Above
Illustration by Eugène Courboin, 1880, for *La Goule es Fées* in *La Bretagne artistique*.

Below
Korrigans, Illustration by Martin de Voos from *The Land of the Elves*.

Above
Illustration by Félix Lorioux, 1923,
In *Quand le fées vivaient en France*.
In Brittany fiendish *korrils* and
poulpiquets prance around standing
stones all night long endlessly reci-
ting the days of the week from
Monday to Saturday. But woe betide the passer-by who lingers and
completes the song by crying out
"Sunday" for he will be instantly
caught up in an infernal round that
ends in his death.

Right
Illustration by Arthur Rackham,
1917, for Grimm's *The Little Gnome*.

In the Shetland Islands, to the north of Scotland, there are evil spirits that have taught musicians to play an infernal tune. Anyone hearing it, no matter how old and infirm, is compelled to join in a dance that continues to the point of exhaustion or even death. To release the spellbound victims, the musician must play the same tune backwards, from the end to the very beginning without a single wrong note.

In Nordic countries the most dreaded demons of all are the *ellicons*, twisted spirits resembling little old men that drag lost travelers into the marshes and push them over precipices. Others jump up onto the saddle behind horsemen seizing the reins and pricking the horses so that they bolt and head for the bogs.

In Norway there is a succubus called Mara that visits lonely men at night to steal their vital energy. The demon enters the house in the form of smoke, seeping into the most draft-proof dwellings through cracks in doors and windows. Once inside, it materializes as an irresistibly beautiful but terribly dangerous woman.

Above
Will-o'-the-wisp.

Will-o'-the-Wisps

Will-o'-the-wisps are the errant souls of dead unbaptized children that appear on October and November nights. A wandering soul is known by a great variety of names including: Fatuus, Friar's Lantern, Jack-o'-Lantern, Wisp, Friar Rush, Fox Fire, Fata Morgana, Fairy Light, Kitty-Candlestick, Meg of the Lantern, Fool's Fire, Dead Man's Candle, Pixie Light and Spunkie. In Flanders, there are will-o'-the-wisps called *doodkeersen* that appear as little skeletons with candles where their hearts should be. Anyone who points their finger at a will-o'-the-wisp will receive a slap on their cheek from an invisible hand.

In England and Scotland there are strange creatures called *bogles* and *boggarts* with an uncanny ability to turn into anything at all in order to outwit humans. Such a creature may appear as a dog, a tree or a saucepan, for instance. But the moment anyone stops to stroke the dog, lie down in the shade of the tree or pick up the saucepan, the *boggart* resumes its original form, jumps onto the back of the luckless victim and digs its claws into their flesh, shrieking with laughter.

The more the terrified victim struggles and tries to escape, the heavier the *bogle* becomes, tightening its hold and only letting go when it has crushed its hapless prey beneath its weight. *Bogles*, *boggarts*, gray men and coppice witches also delight in ambushing lost travelers, breathing pestilential breath into their faces and whispering macabre songs in their ears.

But the most evil of all the goblins are the redcaps, vile wizened old men with hands like talons and iron boots who re-dye their red caps in human blood. They haunt ruined castles in Lowland Scotland, keeping watch from crumbling towers and ancient dungeons for passing travelers who they murder beneath an avalanche of boulders then rush down to dip their caps in the warm, fresh blood. Halloween is also when black elves sharpen flint arrowheads known as elf shot, which they use to attack livestock and sometimes humans too. To protect their livestock from these lethal weapons English peasants would traditionally plow a curved rather than a straight furrow with their oxen. That way, any elves that were aiming for the oxen would be more likely to miss.

Incubi, succubi and nightmares

"I hear an army charging upon the land,
And the thunder of horses plunging; foam about their knees:
Arrogant, in black armour, behind them stand,
Disdaining the reins, with fluttering whips, the Charioteers.

They cry into the night their battle name:
I moan in sleep when I hear afar their whirling laughter.
They cleave the gloom of dreams, a blinding flame,
Clanging, clanging upon the heart as upon an anvil."

James Joyce (1882-1941)

Finally the evil spirits of Halloween come to torment people in their sleep, appearing as incubi or succubi or nightmare demons. The word "nightmare" derives from the old English "mare" or "mær" meaning evil spirit and originally referred to a demon that lay on the stomach of sleeping people, smothering and crushing them under its weight.

A 10th-century Scandinavian legend tells the story of King Vanlandi who returned to Uppsala (in Sweden) after marrying a princess in Finland. Before his departure, the king promised his bride he would return within three years but ten years went by and still the queen had no word from her husband. Lonely and foresaken, she called on the magical powers of the witch Huld who set a curse on Vanlandi summoning the mahr to torment the king as he slept. From that moment forth, night after night, Vanlandi was set upon by the demon that trampled him, crushed his legs, suffocated and in the end killed him.

Nineteenth-century author Colin de Plancy in his *Dictionnaire infernal* gives the following definition of the French word *cauchemar* (from the Dutch *mare* or *mahr* for demon and the old French word *chaucher* for "to weigh down"): "The name given to a sense of restriction or tightness in the chest felt by people as they sleep, making breathing difficult and giving rise to bad dreams that linger on waking. In the 15thcentury when no one fully understood what nightmares were, the simplest thing was to think of them as monsters. For some they were witches or specters that pressed down on the stomachs of sleeping people, gagging and stifling them and preventing them from crying out for help. For others they were demonic incubi that smothered people in the act of sexual intercourse. Doctors were equally vague on the subject of nightmares: all they could suggest to keep them at bay was to hang a hollow stone from the house stables."

Below

Le Monde des spectres.
The Nightmare demon often takes on the appearance of a black elf that suffocates and paralyzes people asleep in the hay. At other times the demon brings death to gluttons by pressing down on their stomachs.

Right

Cauchemar,
Henry Fuseli (1741-1825).
"Eat lightly, do not overload your stomach and avoid sleeping on your back and your incubus will depart with no need of magical incantations or holy water."
Des erreurs et des préjugés, M. Salgues,
(published 1818).

Dwarves and gnomes

Autumn is also a time when the mysterious dwarf people emerge from the bowels of the earth wearing red caps and armed with pickaxes and shovels. Dwarves and gnomes have ugly wizened faces, skin like parchment, bushy beards and their expression may be jovial or scowling. At the end of a hard day's work, they are not averse to a pint of beer and a good pipe. Unlike the youthful springtime faeries and mature summer undines, all dwarves resemble small, misshapen old men, as old as the stones they have been mining in their deep underground galleries since the world began.

Son of the mists

It is told that in their beginning the Dwarves were made
by Aulë in the darkness of Middle-Earth; [...]
He wrought in secret: and he made first the Seven
Fathers of the Dwarves in a hall under the mountains in
Middle-Earth.
The Silmarillion, J.R.R. Tolkien (1892-1973).

Above
Illustration by H.J. Ford
for *The Olive Fairy*.

Right
Illustration by Arthur Rackham,
1917, *for Grimm's Fairytales.*
The dwarves in faerytales are often magical allies placed along the hero's path to help him in his quest. If the hero trusts the small misshapen fellow addressing him he will be spared countless misfortunes. But if he shows contempt for the gnome, the all-powerful midget will wreak a terrible revenge.

According to the *Edda* tales of old Norse mythology, the universe as we know it was formed from the corpse of a primeval giant called Ymir. The earth was made from his flesh, the sea from his blood, the canopy of heaven from his skull, the mountains from his bones and the trees from his hair. When the giant died, the worms that gnawed at his remains turned into the dwarves that were granted human form and intelligence by the gods while continuing to live in the bowels of the earth. Four of them were given the job of supporting the sky on their shoulders. The dwarf people lived in the deep, underground kingdoms of Niflheim, "Land of Mists," and Svartalfaheim, home of the goblins.

Richard Wagner's Ring Cycle, *The Ring of Nibelung*, was inspired by the 13th-century poem *The Niebelungenlied*. It tells the story of the Nibelungen dwarf people and their ruler King Nibelung, "Son of the Mists," who possessed a vast treasure called the Nibelung Hort. This contained magical weapons such as a helmet and cape (the

Tarnhelm and the *Tarnkappe*) that had the power to render the wearer invisible.

The dark mysterious dwarf kingdom could only be entered by way of the Bifrost, a rainbow bridge linking Asgard, the sky, with Midgard, the earth and Niflheim, kingdom of the dwarves, a dark, suffocating region where gods and mortals rarely ventured. For dwarves may indeed be compared to the telluric forces of the underworld and the powers of darkness, death and the beyond. Dwarves are the enemies of light and only at night may they leave their underground kingdom to which they must return at first cock-crow or remain petrified forever by the sun's rays. This explains why some rocks are said to look like grimacing human faces: they are in fact dwarves caught out by the sun and turned to stone. It is also said that dwarves never marry but reproduce by carving rocks in their own image that instantly come alive. The earth is their natural element, the environment where they live and breathe as easily as men live in the air and fish live in water.

DWARVES, THE ARTISANS OF THE EARTH

*"Far from being white and light, they are usually black, hairy, hideous and
thick-set. Their hands are clawed like those of a cat and their feet are thickly
callused. They have wrinkled faces, frizzy hair, small sunken eyes that shine
like boils and their voices are muffled and broken with age."*
From the *Barzaz-Breiz*, a collection of Breton folk songs
published in the mid-nineteenth century by Vicomte
Hersart de la Villemarqué (1815-1895).

Below
On the way to the city of the trolls
Theodor Kittelsen (1857-1914).

Right
Illustration by Heinrich Schlitt
(1849-1923).
In Germany there are mountain dwarves known as the Erdluitle or "People of the Earth" that have existed for much longer than men and know the secrets of Nature. Their skin is the color of the earth, their hair is black and they wear green, blue and gray overalls that hide their webbed feet of which they are ashamed and would never expose under any circumstances.

In Lower Brittany, where dwarves dig burrows beneath standing stones and megaliths, dolmens are known locally as *ty-corriked* (house of the dwarves) or *loch-corriganed* (dwarf lodge). Dwarves are intensely house-proud and sweep their homes every night without fail. Some dwarves, such as the diminutive *berstuc* and *koltk* which are barely one or two inches tall, cling to the roots of trees or ploughed soil or take a nap in the shade of a blade of grass. Dwarves are reclusive and rather grumpy by nature and, although they keep out of sight as much as possible, they may sometimes be glimpsed on the borders of woods, creeping through the undergrowth, crossing deserted moors or disappearing into cracks in the rocks. They are equally sensitive to cold and intense heat and much prefer the temperate environment of their subterranean world, sheltered from the extremes of weather that are typical of what they call "the world outside" where they only venture in autumn to gather their annual supplies of mushrooms, walnuts and chestnuts.

Whether good or bad, all dwarves posses magical powers. They are also hard-working and

How dwarves breathe

"Just as we know that there are four elements – air, water, earth and fire – so we also know that we mortal men are born of Adam, that we stand upright and walk through the air just as fish swim through water and that we can no more do without air than fish can do without water. [...] It is the same with the mountain gnomes. The earth is like their air and acts as their vital element, for each thing exists in its vital element. Thus the earth is nothing other than the vital element of the mountain dwarves since, like spirits, they can pass through solid walls, rocks and stones. [...].

Indeed, for the mountain dwarves the earth is their vital element. It is the very air that they breathe and not like the earth it is for us.

It follows that they can see through earth just as we can see through air and that sunlight reaches them through earth as it reaches us through air, and that they, just like us, can see the sun, the moon and the heavenly firmament. It is the same with the undines that have water as their vital element: for them, water is no obstacle to the sun; on the contrary, just as the sun reaches us through air, so it reaches them through water. It is the same with the vulcans that can see through fire. Note also that they like us depend on the sun for light which makes the land fertile and that they too therefore have summer and winter, day and night."

Paracelsus.

the absolute masters of the soil and subsoil, supervising the germination of plants, excavating tunnels in search of minerals, watching over deposits of precious stones and guarding buried treasure. They are painfully over-sensitive and any offence – such as mocking their diminutive size or webbed feet – will surely meet with retribution in the form of mischievous tricks or sometimes acts of extreme violence. But provided you know how to handle them and coax them with gifts and flattery, then they can be steadfast allies.

119

Goldsmith dwarves

Dwarves are master goldsmiths, capable of producing exquisite jewelry that no human artisan, however gifted, could ever rival. They are also formidable blacksmiths whose swords are so strong and light that they render the bearer invincible. The fabulous Durandal was a sword so robust it could split the mountain in two without shattering. It was forged for the hero Roland by a dwarf called Wieland (or Geland) assisted by other dwarves from the mountain of Kallowa. Other legendary swords made by dwarves were the Doolen of Mayence and especially the infamous sword Dainsleif that "shall be a man's bane every time it is drawn; and its stroke never strays from the target, and the wound dealt by it never heals" (from *The Saga of King Heidrek the Wise*, translated by Christopher Tolkien, 1960).

Opposite and right
Illustration by Arthur Rackham for *The Rhine Gold*, 1910.
The dwarf Wieland was a gifted goldsmith who was captured by a queen and imprisoned on an island in the middle of a lake after first having the tendons in his legs severed to stop him from escaping. The queen's intention was to keep the dwarf's talents for herself. But Wieland took his revenge by chopping off the heads of the royal children then using the skulls to make two exquisite ivory goblets which he then had delivered to the queen before flying away using a pair of golden wings that he had forged in secret.

Following double page
The Altar Cup in Aagerup,
Richard Doyle.

The prophecy of the gnomes

*"In my fire tonight, a pretty gnome with a gol-
den belt whispers sweet nothings into the ear of
a pretty salamander as she falls asleep."*
Le Brandon, Tristan Klingsor
(1874-1966).

Among the many different families of dwarves, the most knowledgeable are the gnomes whose name comes from the Greek *gnômé* meaning "intelligence." Their prophetic ability is all-seeing and they are the custodians of all the wisdom and learning in the world. So knowledgeable are they indeed that King Solomon himself would frequently consult gnomes before passing judgment. According to the Talmud and the Cabala, one of these gnomes is reported to have applied his knowledge of sacred architecture to the building of the Temple of Jerusalem.

This is what Karl Grün has to say on the subject of gnomes: "According to the Jewish Cabala, the gnome knows all the secrets of the Earth; it is he who brings life to all living creatures and he who takes it away when he departs. There was once a time when the gnome was mischievous but good-natured; whereas today he has become nasty and ugly. His wife, the gnomide, who is even smaller than he is but ravishingly beautiful and superbly dressed, makes no sound when she walks except for the soft padding of her jeweled slippers, one emerald and one ruby. Gnomides usually have the job of guarding precious gems. Some gnomes are not only small but so minutely proportioned that they can slip through cracks in the ground in crystalline caves sparkling with long green stalactites. They sleep lightly beneath a canopy of gold and silver."

Gnomes are also the custodians of buried treasure, as explained here by Paracelsus: "The Lord appoints guardians of Nature to watch over all things and leaves nothing unguarded. Thus do the gnomes, the pygmies and the spirits of the dead mount guard over the treasures of the Earth which are the base metals and other minerals. For where these spirits reside exist vast deposits of considerable treasure that the creatures guard and conceal from our view lest we should discover them before the time has come. When we do discover them we say: "Once there were dwarves and gnomes in this mountain but now that time has gone." Which is as if to say that the time has come to reveal the Earth's riches. For the Earth's treasures are distributed in such a way that ever since the world began we have gradually come to discover the base metals, silver, gold, iron and so forth that the creatures have been guarding and watching over so that they should not be discovered all at once but one by one and little by little, now in one country, now in another. Thus do the mines change place with time and from country to another, in chronological order from the first day to the last."

But for all their wisdom and learning, these wealthy, powerful and omniscient gnomes can often be puffed up with pride and full of malice. Indeed they are said to have regular dealings with the Devil and all his acolytes to which they are closely related. For these formidable gnomes live in immense underground towns deep in the bowels of the earth from whence they only emerge when forced by a tyrannical magus, or to attend that sinister cavorting of evil faerie spirits that gather on the night of Halloween.

Left
Illustration by E. Fortescue Brickdale (1871-1945).
Gnomes know the whereabouts of buried treasure that they willingly reveal to worthy mortals who they think will make proper use of it. In most cases however, the humans enriched by the Good People's generosity suddenly turn greedy and grasping. So gnomes these days hardly ever appear to humans except perhaps to gentle virgins who remain innocent in the ways of the world.

Right
The Gnome (1928), Marjorie Miller.

Giants

In most mythologies, giants are primeval beings whose origins date back to when the world began. In Greek mythology for instance, the titans, the giants and the Cyclops were the fruit of the union of the Earth and sky. But these formidably powerful, crude and brutal creatures fought murderous, fratricidal battles which none of them survived.

In Norse mythology, the enemies of the gods were a race of colossal beings born of the sweat of the giant Ymir and called the "Giants of the Frost." Odin and his brothers eventually slew Ymir who was a threat to their omnipotence but the blood that gushed from his wounds drowned all of the giants except for one. The gods then used the remains of the slaughtered Ymir to create the World as we know it. From his blood, they made the sea and the lakes; from his flesh they modeled the earth; with his bones they built the mountains; and with his teeth they made the rocks and stones. His skull became the celestial canopy, his brain gave rise to the clouds, his hair became the trees and his eyelashes, planted like fence posts, marked the borders of Midgard, the world of men. In the same way, the Fomorians who first inhabited Ireland were terrifying giants who merged with the mists, the thunder and the winter. Many regions of France and Switzerland are witness to the passage of the mythical giant Gargantua who is said to have dug Lake Geneva and the Saône riverbed while erecting countless peaks along the way, especially the Mont-Saint-Michel formerly known as "Mont Tombe" or "Mont Gargan." The Napoleonic author Thomas de Saint-Mars describes the giant in *Gargantua au pays de Retz* as an 18th-century gentleman taller than the tallest tree, who carried his staff and servants in his pockets. On each stage of his journey, he devoured a hundred loaves each weighing 18 lbs. and drained a dozen barrels of wine. Then the good giant would sleep for two whole days before setting off again. In Paris, it was his wont to sit astride the towers of Notre Dame cathedral and dip his feet into the waters of the River Seine below. According to some legends, Gargantua's parents, Grangosier and Galemelle, were created by the sorcerer Merlin from a variety of ingredients: a flask of Lancelot's blood, nail clippings from King Arthur's wife Guinevere and the bones of two whales. Gargantua is even believed to have crossed the English Channel to offer his services at the court of King Arthur. He remained in the service of the king for 200 years, three months and four days before being carried off to the land of Faerie by the faeries Morgana and Melusina.

Fasolt und Fafnir,
illustration by Franz Stassen
from *The Rhine Gold*
The giants were essentially
builders to whom we owe not
just the mountains and valleys,
fields and rivers but also castles,
towns and fortifications. Asgard,
the impregnable dwelling place
of the gods, was built by the
giants Fasolt and Fafnir.

SIF'S GOLDEN LOCKS AND THOR'S HAMMER

Only the cunning Loki, god of Fire, was an habitué at the court of the dwarves, whom he often asked for assistance. One day he called on the skills of two talented dwarves to forge him a golden head of hair for Sif, wife of Thor, the god of Thunder. Sif's real hair was in shreds after being maliciously chopped off by Loki. But the new artificial hair was so supple and silky that it looked just the real thing and once it had taken root in the scalp it would grow just like real hair too.

But the dwarves of Niflheim, anxious to find favor in the eyes of the gods and win their praise and recognition, did much more than forge a golden head of hair for Sif. They also built a fabulous craft called the *Skidbladnir* that fitted into a small pouch when dismantled but was large enough when fully assembled to accommodate all of the gods. Next they forged the lance Gungnir, an enchanted weapon that never missed its target, and offered it to Odin, god of gods.

Meanwhile the brothers Brokk and Eitri, determined not to be outdone in creativity, offered a golden boar called Gullinbursti to Freyr, the god of Earth's fertility. The magical pig could travel through the airs and the seas at the speed of a horse while illuminating the blackest darkness with the reflected light from its golden bristles. Then they forged a magical ring that every ninth night turned into eight identical gold rings. Finally they created a hammer called Mjollnir and presented it as a gift to Thor. The god had only to throw the hammer and it would strike any obstacle without shattering before returning to the hand of its owner. Everyone agreed that this was the dwarves' greatest achievement, although all these magical gifts were much appreciated by the gods of Asgard, who were quick to sing their praises.

The divinations of the Little People

"The reason for the existence of mermaids, giants, dwarves and will-o'-the-wisps is that they predict and indicate something new. Their role is not that of guardians but their presence is of dire portent to human beings. When there are will-o'-the-wisps abroad, the country's downfall is at hand. Generally their presence portends the collapse of the monarchy or other such things. Giants too are harbingers of appalling devastation to land and territory or other equally calamitous events. Dwarves usually foretell of great poverty among the people while mermaids augur the overthrow of lords and princes and the formation of sects and parties. For the Lord God wishes to preserve us in our unique essence and wipes out all those who stand in His way: and when that time shall come to pass, there will be signs and auguries among which shall be these creatures."

PARACELSUS

Illustration by Gustave Doré, 1857.

Ogres and bogeymen

Ogres and ogresses are giants that eat human flesh, their favorite food being plump young children's bodies. These bloodthirsty monsters are usually powerful overlords with immense wealth and lands and countless castles. Each of the ogres in *Puss in Boots* and *Tom Thumb* was the heir to untold fortunes in goods and fabulous riches, but their grasping, narrow-minded nature led them straight into the traps that were set for them by their smaller adversaries. Ogres are therefore the symbols of a brute force that must be channeled and refined before it can reveal its true worth. Among the dark legions of ogres, one of the most infamous is the bogeyman that carries off disobedient children to devour them. These malevolent creatures of folklore range from merely troublesome and rather harmless to truly evil. They also change shape at will, displace objects and generally cause havoc. Although a bogeyman usually haunts a family, it can occasionally make friends with individual members and even become a playmate for the children. The bogle is a more evil type of bogeyman, although this

one usually only harms liars and murderers. A bogeymen is vague and amorphous in appearance, resembling a large puff of dust. He can be spotted by looking quickly through a knothole in a wooden partition. If a bogeyman is on the other side, you might catch the dull gleam of his eye before he has time to move away. The name "Bogeymen" may be derived from the *bugis* who were evil pirates from Indonesia and Malaysia. English and French sailors returned home with tales of the bugis' heinous doings, telling their children that the pirates would come and get them if they misbehaved. It is conceivable that bugis eventually developed into bogey and then bogeyman. In France, bogeymen are known as *croquemitaines* which literally means "mitten eaters." The original Croquemitaine is said to have been the son of Gargantua who christened his progeny the mitten-eater because as a child he had no teeth and all he could eat were woolen mittens. But according to another source, Croquemitaine was not a child-eater at all but a cat lover who occasionally ate the objects of his affections!

The wolf Fenrir and the blood of Kvasir

Loki's love affair with the giant Angrboda had spawned three children: the monstrous wolf Fenrir which it had been predicted would one day snap up the world in his iron jaws; the terrible Midgard sea serpent; and Hel, the female guardian of the resting place of the dead located deep in the bowels of Niflheim. To shackle Fenrir, that no normal bonds could restrain, the gods of Asgard once again called on the skillful dwarves who forged a magical restraint called Gleipnir from six highly exotic ingredients: the soft padding of a cat's paws, women's beards, the roots of mountains, wolves' tendons, fish breath and bird saliva.

The inhabitants of Niflheim were also the custodians of the secrets of runic poetry that they revealed to Odin. The *Edda* tells the tale of how the dwarves set a trap for Kvasir, advisor to the gods, by luring him into their underground kingdom. Such was Kvasir's reputation for wisdom that the dwarves decided to appropriate it for themselves using black magic. They cut Kvasir's throat and filled two basins and a cauldron with his blood that they mixed with honey to make the mead of poetry. But the dwarves had killed the parents of the giant Suttung and, to escape his vengeance, they were forced to flee leaving behind the elixir of wisdom and poetry that passed into the hands of the gods. Since then only the gods can dispense this precious beverage to mortals who have won their favors.

Below
Loki, an illustration by F. Stassen from the *Edda*.
Loki, god of Fire, was willful and fickle, playing endless tricks on the other gods who mistrusted him in particular because of his known associations with Niflheim, the dark kingdom of the dwarves.

Herla and the King of the Dwarves

King Herla, the noble and valiant sovereign of the Isle of Brittany, was preparing to marry the most beautiful woman in his kingdom. Three days before the wedding ceremony he was hunting wild boar when he spotted an old male with white hair that he swore to hunt down and kill before returning to the castle.

The boar was a magical animal for the ancient Bretons and the white boar in particular was a fabulous creature that no hunter in the world would have allowed to escape.

But what happened next stopped Herla dead in his tracks. There before him was a misshapen little man wearing a green mantlet and red cap with a face that seemed to have been carved in the bark of a tree. It was the King of the Dwarves.

Herla knew that the dwarves are a proud and very sensitive people with magical, sometimes evil powers. So he greeted the diminutive sovereign with a flourish, ostentatiously sweeping his hat to the ground.

"Greetings, O King of the Dwarves! Your presence on my lands does me great honor. Such an encounter must be a sign of good fortune!" Herla knew that although the dwarves are a proud and sensitive people they respond well to flattery and fawning. He fully expected his well-turned compliment to meet with the kinglet's approval. How wrong he was! Instead, the dwarf king scowled beneath his bushy eyebrows and snarled between gritted teeth: "What makes you think that? Is it superstition? Have you read somewhere that meeting a dwarf is a sign of luck? Would you say the same had you come across a mere human just like you? Well, answer me! Am I just one of nature's aberrations in your eyes? A freak show, a monster? A good luck charm like a four-leafed clover? Well I'm not, see, I'm a dwarf! And not just any dwarf, but the King of the Dwarves!"

The little king's craggy face turned positively puce with rage but before he could continue his ranting Herla replied: "You do me wrong, O King of the Dwarves! My respect for you knows no bounds, it is as great as your ... as your bravery ... And once again, I bless the hand of destiny that placed you in my path because ..."

"What's all this rubbish about destiny! I'm the one who decided to come and meet you, King Herla, to insist on an explanation!"

"Explanation? What explanation, O wise King of the Dwarves?"

"It's no use playing the innocent with me, Herla, and you can wipe that toadying grin off your face too! Need I remind you that it's your wedding day three days from now? Perhaps you'd like me to refresh your memory by reeling off the names of all the lords and nobles you've invited to the ceremony? All the nobility on the Isle of Brittany will be there — except for me, the King of the Dwarves! Do you not think me worthy to be your guest, is that it? Are dwarves not allowed to attend the weddings of the good and great of this world?"

Herla felt himself blench. It was true, he had forgotten to invite the King of the Dwarves. Quick, he had to find a way to make up for such an appalling oversight. "A thousand pardons, O powerful King of the Dwarves. It must be the fault of my chamberlain — whose head shall roll when I return. Believe me, your presence matters more to me than anything in the world ... I beg you to do me the honor of attending my wedding three days from now, in the company of your most valiant dwarf knights! You shall be treated with all the respect ... all the respect ... You shall be treated with the greatest of dignity!"

The little king puffed up with pride at Herla's words and replied: "Very well, in that case I am prepared to do you the honor of attending your wedding. I shall be with you three days hence accompanied by my finest dwarf knights. But for the present, I bid you good night ..."

And with these words, the midget king

disappeared into thin air. Herla headed home deep in thought, having forgotten all about the white boar.

The wedding ceremony was celebrated three days later with the pomp and circumstance befitting such an occasion. All of the noble lords and ladies of the Isle of Brittany were there – not forgetting, of course, the King of the Dwarves and his knights. The following three days and three nights were given over to music and dancing, juggling, drinking and story-telling.

When the three days and nights were ended, the King of the Dwarves approached the throne and bowed proudly before the royal couple. Then he took his leave with these words: "Thank you for your welcome, King Herla, but now I must return to my kingdom – where I await you eight days from now, together with your finest knights, so that I may have the honor of returning your hospitality. See you in eight days time then! And whatever you do, don't be late! Kings do not like to be kept waiting and dwarves even less. As for the King of the Dwarves ..."

And in an instant, the little king and his knights vanished in a puff of smoke. The new queen pleaded with her husband to turn down the dwarf's invitation but it was no use. "Sweet wife, I cannot refuse the dwarf's invitation without provoking his anger and incurring his vengeance. I shall go, but I shall not tarry. I shall remain with the dwarf three days and nights but not a moment longer. You have my word upon it!"

Eight days later, Herla and his finest knights set off on horseback for the dwarf king's palace. They had to ride right across the kingdom because the midget's palace nestled within a distant mountain that could only be entered through a slim crack in the rock.

Herla and his knights left their horses outside and ventured into the narrow entrance. They soon reached an immense cave that seemed to be in broad daylight although the light was apparently coming from the rock itself. The walls of the cave were hung with the finest examples of dwarf craftsmanship: legendary swords, magical weapons, beautifully engraved jewelry and golden necklaces.

In the center of the hall was the King of the Dwarves with his subjects who welcomed Herla and his company of knights with goblets brimful of brown ale, plates loaded with roasted boar, tobacco pouches filled with the finest pipe tobacco and musicians playing the bagpipes. The following three days and three nights were given over to music and dancing, juggling, drinking and story-telling.

At the end of the three days and three nights, King Herla approached the King of the Dwarves to take his leave.

"Surely you're not thinking of leaving so soon?" growled the King of the Dwarves. "The festivities have only just started. Here they last for a very long time — a very long time indeed!"

"Yes, but my wife awaits me, O King of the Dwarves. Don't forget that I am recently married. I long to visit her bed that she may bear me handsome offspring." And the king laughed raucously, failing to notice the look of hatred and envy that flashed in the dwarf king's eyes. "Well off you go then, King Herla," said the midget. "Run along home and be sure to remember me to your wife. Ha, ha."

The mockery in the dwarf king's laughter made Herla's blood run cold. Without further ado, he and his escort left the hall and the underground palace and returned to the open air.

Once outside, they found that their own horses had disappeared. In their place were dwarf horses that grew to normal size when they were mounted. Herla then gave the signal to depart and the company set off at a gallop.

But there were a few surprises in store for the king of Brittany. Where three days earlier there had been forests, there were now meadows and cultivated fields. The wooden huts in the villages had been replaced by stone houses. The peasants wore strange clothes and spoke in a dialect that neither Herla nor his escort could understand.

Soon they came within sight of the castle — only to find that it was in ruins!

Just then, Herla spotted an old shepherd nearby and called him over to ask news of his wife, the beautiful queen of the Bretons whom he had left alone in the castle just a few days earlier. The shepherd looked at the king with amazement then replied: "I have difficulty understanding you, my lord, because I am a Saxon and you speak the tongue of the ancient Bretons. The queen you speak of was the wife of King Herla, former king of the Bretons who is said to have left his kingdom barely eight days after his wedding never to be seen again. They say he went off to the kingdom of the dwarves in some far-off distant mountain. It's probably only a legend but, if true, it happened nearly three centuries ago, just before the Saxons invaded Brittany and drove out all the inhabitants.

King Herla who thought he had only been absent three days had in fact spent three centuries in the dwarf kingdom. In that time, his wife had died of a broken heart, his subjects had been exiled and he was now all alone in the world, bereft of country and family.

One of the knights made to dismount but the instant his foot touched the ground he crumbled to ashes. For the horses they had been given by the dwarf king were magic and Herla and his knights remained alive only for so long as they remained seated. But they would turn to dust should they be tempted to dismount.

Since that fateful day, King Herla and his men have roamed the Isle of Brittany, endlessly wandering the woods and moors, doomed to ride till the end of time. Sometimes, especially on dark stormy nights beneath lowering skies, their black silhouettes are visible against the horizon. People say then that it's King Herla and his men out hunting, lost souls forever bereft of peace of mind and body.

The festival of light

The great winter night has the whole world in its freezing clutches. The naked trees shiver in the desolate woods and gardens. Most of the denizens of Faerie are hibernating, waiting for spring. No airy faery in the woods. No mischievous elfin chorus. No languishing siren on the deserted strand. Even the autumn dwarves have returned to their underground shelters. Are we to believe that winter is not a time for faery creatures? No, thank goodness, because however icy and inhospitable, winter features an oasis of joy and light: Christmas!

Before it became a Christian event, Christmas or Yuletide was a very ancient pagan festival linked to the rites of the winter solstice on the twenty-first day of December, a few days before Christmas. At the winter solstice, the sun is so low in the sky and the days so short that the shadows of darkness threaten to take over the world forever. On these long cold nights that mark the start of winter, to conjure their fear of the dark people would gather by the fire around a fir tree festooned with garlands and twinkling candles. In some regions, the evergreen fir tree covered with multicolored ornaments resembling the fruits of heaven is also known as the "Christmas May Tree." For Christmas, with its hope of spring, is a celebration of the light and passion that will rise anew from the ashes of winter.

Let us now see how it is traditionally celebrated in different parts of the world.

Garlands of flowers and fays

In many regions of France, it is the tradition on Christmas night to make offerings to the sprites and undines that dwell in springs and wells. In Brittany people throw bouquets of flowers and fruit into the water to keep it clear all year round.

In Provence, in southeast France, every housewife drawing water from the well leaves humble offerings around the edges: a hunk of bread, a piece of shortbread, cakes or goat's cheese. The next woman to come along takes these gifts and leaves similar gifts of her own, as does the woman after her until, by nightfall, all the women in the village have exchanged presents blessed by the faeries. These Yuletide gifts are regarded as good luck charms and stored in a safe place.

On Christmas Eve in the Béarn, in southwest France, faeries or fays known locally as "*blanquettes*" are said to visit every home. They carry two children in their arms, one crowned with flowers symbolizing good luck and one in tears symbolizing bad luck. It is the tradition on that night to prepare a quiet bedroom where no one is allowed to sleep, and leave some bread and wine, a glass and a lighted candle on a table covered with a white table cloth. If the faeries feel honored by these attentions they will leave behind the child crowned with flowers, so bringing the family good luck. But if they feel hard done by, they will leave behind the child in tears and throughout the coming year the family will be dogged by misfortune.

The following morning, being Christmas Day, the master of the house and all his family enter the *blanquettes'* bedroom. He breaks the bread set aside for the good faeries and dips a piece in the wine that he pours into the glass. Then he shares out the rest of the bread among all the people present who wish each other a Happy New Year and go and eat the bread blessed by the faeries for their breakfast. In the Berry, in northern France, Christmas night is also the devil's night when Satan is said to take advantage of the Lord's nativity to tempt the faithful on their way to midnight mass. Suddenly the paths and crossroads are scattered with devil's gold that glitters irresistibly in the pitch-black night. Gaping caverns appear at the foot of crucifixes, chapels and wayside crosses, overflowing with gold and precious gems. But woe betide anyone who helps themselves to these ill-gotten gains, for they will be instantly plunged into hell.

Au gui l'an neuf

"For tall forests do as
surely attract miracles as tall trees
do attract the lightening."
La Forêt de Brocéliande, Félix Bellamy
(late 19th-century author).

In the ancient country of Gaul, the winter solstice was the time when the Druids would cut the sacred mistletoe with their golden scythes. This ceremony, linked with the cult of the sun god Belenos, was accompanied by the words *"Au gui l'an neuf"* ("Mistletoe for the New Year"), a New Year greeting that is still heard today, centuries later. The Druids believed that mistletoe had miraculous properties and any enemies meeting under the mistletoe in the forest had to lay down their arms and observe a day's truce. This may be the origin of the ancient custom of hanging a bouquet of mistletoe from the ceiling and exchanging kisses under it as a sign of friendship and goodwill. This custom, which was widespread among the Anglo-Saxons and survives today in many European countries as well as in Canada, might equally be connected to the legend of Freya, goddess of love, beauty and fertility. If lovers exchange a kiss under

· FAIRY · PRINCESS ·

Christmas Visitors

Befana, festival of Epiphany

*"One, two, three hundred rats,
here comes the Befana!"*
Italian nursery rhyme.

Below
In Italy at the Feast of the Epiphany people see out the old year and bring in the new with the ritual burning of the Befana in effigy.

In Italy there is a witch called the Befana who streaks across the sky on her broomstick taking presents to children at Epiphany. People say that she was originally a widow who earned her living gathering firewood. Then one day the Three Magi passed by her house and invited her to accompany them to Bethlehem to worship the infant Jesus. But the Befana was old and poor and declined their invitation. When the Magi had left she regretted her decision and after bringing in her firewood so that no-one would steal it, she set off to catch them up carrying a sack full of toys on her back. But she had left it too late and lost her way.

The exhausted Befana wandered all over Europe, badly dressed, all in black, her face covered in soot and her feet stuffed into enormous shoes. Eventually she found refuge in Italy where ever since then to make up for being late, she sets off on the night of 5-6 January to distribute nice presents to children who have been good, and horrid presents to children who have been horrid. But good or bad, Italian children love her almost as much as they love Father Christmas. It was once the custom in Italy to build a sort of gigantic rag-doll effigy of the Befana, with a grotesque head and absurdly long, wavy arms, and sit her in a cart alongside other ridiculous characters. The cart would then parade around the town before eventually heading for the town square where the Befana was put on a bonfire and burned in effigy.

Above
The Befana,
20th-century illustration.

BABUSHKA, FATHER FROST AND THE SNOW FAERY

"Little mother Babushka, protect me from Baba-Yaga's whip."
Russian nursery rhyme.

In Russia there is a similar legend about an old woman called Babushka who also received a visit from the Three Magi but hesitated because of the cold. When she finally did set off, all trace of the Magi's sleigh tracks had been covered over by the snow. After knocking in vain at all the doors, she wandered the frozen steppes of Russia, her pockets full of black bread which was all she possessed in the world. The story doesn't say whether she reached Bethlehem in the end. Since then though, in memory of the Babushka's long journey, it is the custom in Russia to offer children black bread at Christmas, so calling on the good grandmother to protect them from the wicked witch Baba-Yaga by chanting nursery rhymes.

People also say that on the night of the Epiphany Russian homes are visited by Father Frost who leaves presents in the hearths. With him is his pretty teenage daughter, Sniegourotshka, the Snow Faery, made entirely of snow but as alive as you and me, who travels in a sleigh drawn by three magnificent horses.

Opposite
Father Frost, illustration by Ivan Bilibine (1876-1942) for *Contes de l'Isba*. Sniegourotshka, the Snow Faery, is the daughter of Father Frost, the Russian equivalent of our Father Christmas whose names include Père Noël in France, Kriss Kringle in Germany, and Santa Claus in North America (where he was originally called Sinter Claus by settlers who first came to New York from Germany).

Left
Baba Yaga on her mortar, illustration by Ivan Bilibine for *Contes de l'Isba*.

149

The Faery Berchta, Dame Holle and Tante Arie

In the south of Germany, it is a faery of Nordic descent called Berchta that does the rounds with the presents on the sixth night of January. For the rest of the year she follows Odin on his desperate hunt for Asgard. In the north, people are more inclined to believe that the present giver is Dame Holle. In eastern France, it is Tante Arie, the Air Faery assisted by her lady present-bearers who check that the house is neat and tidy before leaving their precious gifts. They pay particular attention to looms and spinning wheels which symbolize the cycles and new beginnings associated with this time of year.

The faery Bertha and her servants

"The temporary goddesses,
the winter ladies and the Christmas aunties,
Advent, Christmas and Epiphany,
Are so many doors to the Great Kingdom."
L'Esprit des fées, Angélus Milhauset.

In Franche-Comté, in eastern France, it is the faery Bertha who visits homes every year at midnight in the week between Christmas and the Day of Circumcision (the first day of January). Bertha the Spinner is descended from Bertha of Burgundy who would wind a distaff of flax every day to set an example. The faery Bertha now ranks as the queen of the good faeries and the guardian of domestic virtues. She visits households with a magic wand in one hand and a distaff in the other, and woe betide any woman who through laziness or negligence has forgotten to spin her flax. Bertha will surely tangle it so tightly that it is no longer fit for spinning.

Elsewhere, she orders her servants, little household Brownies, to pull the covers off lazy people still abed, to cause the slatternly, unkempt cow girl to drop her jug of milk and to punish untidy, spendthrift peasants by wringing the neck of their fattest cow. But when Bertha and her faithful little servants come across a well-kept house, with clean linen neatly stored in old wooden chests, spotless bedrooms and floors swept clean of loose flax, then she sets to work. In the morning, the deserving housewife wakes to find that her brass has been polished, her floors freshly waxed, her chimney swept and her hearth emptied of cinders. To thank Bertha the Spinner and her faithful servants the grateful lady leaves a hunk of bread and a pitcher of water on the kitchen table or by the hearth.

Right
Illustration by Otto Gebhardt.

Opposite
Father Whipper, otherwise known as Hans Trapp. Since the 12th century, a disguised Saint Nicolas has gone from house to house on the night of the fifth day of December to reward good children with gifts of toys and candy. Naughty children on the other hand get a whipping from the saint's companion, father Whipper before being hoisted into his hod and carried off.

Hans Trapp and the Good Child

In Austria, Switzerland and some parts of Germany, it is the Christkindle – the Christ Child – the infant Jesus Himself, who does the rounds at Epiphany, although He is not the one who comes down the chimney. He is assisted by a young teenager wearing a crown of candles and dressed in white, and a bogeyman called Hans Trapp or Ruppelz. One hands out presents and candy, the other dishes out smacks and chastisements. For children who have misbehaved, the supreme punishment is to be hoisted into the wicker basket that the ogre carries on his back. In the Swiss canton of Vaud, Father Christmas is known as the "Bon Enfant" ("Good Child") and does his rounds seated on a donkey. Not so long ago presents were only given on New Year's Day while for Christmas

children in the Vaud had to content themselves with cornets of walnuts or hazelnuts. But the Bon Enfant is not the only visitor at Christmas time. There is also the wicked witch Chauchevieille (a close relative of the Nightmare demon or *"Cauchemar"* as she is known locally) that wanders from house to house on a blind horse and dressed in rags, ready to play nasty tricks and cast spells on naughty children. Like the Befana and the other Christmas faeries, Chauchevieille rewards children who have been good and punishes those who have misbehaved by carrying them off with her. She and the Bon Enfant now work as a team in the canton of Vaud, the witch filling the hod with presents and birch rods and the Bon Enfant taking care of delivery.

Right and following
Illustration of Hans Trapp and the
Bon Enfant by Paul Hey (1867-1952).

THE GREAT BANQUET OF YULE

When the time comes for the great banquet of Yule, men fire shots into the air to chase away evil spirits. At the end of the feast however, the demons are given the leftovers as a token of appeasement. People must also remember to leave all their brooms outside where the witches can find them and fly off to the Brocken to take part in the Sabbath that is presided over by Old Nick, the Devil himself. Woe betide the household that forgets to leave its brooms outside because the witches will break into the stables and steal the oxen and horses.

All night long, the door to the scullery must be left open so that the faery Huedren, the Woman of the Woods, can come in and have something to eat. Also, when serving the traditional Christmas porridge known as the *julegroden*, people always set aside a helping for the *nisse* or resident pixie, then leave it by the hearth or outside the barn door where the pixie is sure to tuck in with relish.

CHRISTMAS WITCHES AND GHOSTS

"There must have been a dozen there, all eating their beer gruel,
and each one ate with a spoon made from the bone of a dead
man's forearm."
Gaspard de la nuit, Louis (alias Aloysius)
Bertrand (1807-1841).

On the night of the Winter Solstice, the skies are filled with the sound of galloping horses as Odin and his knights pursue their hunt for Asgard. His followers are dead men who do not deserve to go to hell for this sins but nor do they deserve to go to heaven. Their punishment is to gallop through the skies until Judgment Day, mounted on black horses with blazing eyes.

Above
Illustration by Hans Gabriel
Jentzsch,1862.

Opposite
The ride of the Valkyries,
illustration by William T. Maud.

Right
The Valkyries, illustration
by Hermann Hendrich, 1924.
"So we abandoned the former god Odin
and his company, but everything that was
once attributed to him and everything that used
to be done in his honor such as, among other
things, leaving the last ear of corn for his horse,
now shifted partly to Saint Nicolas; we moun-
ted the bishop on a horse, gave him a black
valet with a whip and a bag of cinders and cal-
led them Saint Nicolas the Demon."
Rond den Herd, Guido Guezelle.

The Yuletide Tomte or Christmas elf

In Germanic and Nordic countries where the winters are particularly long and cruel, it used to be the tradition at Christmas time to hang the pines in the forest with baskets of food and offerings in honor of the *juls*, the Nordic elves that live in the trees. People would then set fire to a huge wreathe of twisted pine branches symbolizing the wheel of the sun and roast a wild boar on the embers for the grand midnight feast of Yuletide, an Old Norse pagan festival in which the fires and festivities sought to hasten the long-awaited return of the light.

In northern European countries, especially Sweden and her neighbors, it is widely known that every year on the night of the solstice, the Yule *Tomte* or Christmas elf goes to the top of the highest mountain in the country to fetch back the sun. In the morning, the tomte returns with small branches of green and red holly pinned to his chest. The Yule Tomte is like a miniature version of Father Christmas that brings people the finest gift of all: the new light.

The twelve nights separating Christmas from the feast of the Epiphany is a magical time when dreams come true and all of the good and bad events that will punctuate the twelve months to come are prefigured, including the weather.

Left
Yule Tomte, anonymous illustration for an early 12th-century calendar.
"The twelve days between Christmas and the feast of the Epiphany foretell the weather in the twelve months to come."

Below
Le Tomte, engraving by L. Fillol.

Winter elves

*"It ganne to rayne, the kinge and Queene they runne
Under a mushroom fretted over head
With Glowormes, Artificially doune,
Resembling much the canopy of a bedd
Of cloth of silver: and such glimmeringe light
It gave, as stars doe in a frosty night."*
From a Jacobean poem, *The Sports of the Fairies.*

Right
Illustration by Félix Lorioux.

Below
Söndags-Nisse, Swedish satirical journal, January 1884.
In Iceland, the *tomtes* and *nisses* gave rise to the 13 little Christmas visitors known as the Jolasveinar: Stekkjastaur (bearer of a fence post); Giljagaur, (who howls in gorges); Stufur (the tiny one); Thusrusleikir (the ladle licker); Pottaskefill (the pan scraper); Askameikir (the milk-curd licker); Hurdaskellir (the door slammer); Skyrjarmur (who clamors for his bowl of milk); Bjugnakrachir (the sausage thief); Gluggagaegir (the window peeper); Gattathefur (the doorway sniffer); Ketkrokur (the meat thief); and Kedasnikir (the candle thief).

The *tomtes* are found mainly in Sweden and Norway while their relatives the *nisses* are more common in Denmark, Finland, along the Baltic coast and in the Faeroes, where they are known as *niägruisar*. They resemble smiling little old men with round, wrinkled faces, long white beards and red caps. It is they who come down the chimney on Christmas night, bearing presents for well-behaved children. As a reward, it is the custom to leave them a glass of milk by the hearth and a pinch of snuff. But these little Nordic household divinities are not content with distributing presents on Christmas night. They also look after the running of the house and the well-being of its occupants. A home protected by a *tomte* or a *nisse* is easily recognizable because everything is neat and tidy and there is an immediate sense of beauty and harmony.

These resident imps love to dance and act and they are outstanding musicians, with a particular talent for the violin. But they hate disorder and sudden noise. They also do duty as the guardian angels of children who they shield from danger and act as their confidants, teachers and even travelling companions. It was a *tomte* for instance that accompanied Nils Holgersson, the young hero in the novel by Selma Lagerlöf, on his journey across Sweden.

Goblin Harvest, 1910
attributed to Amelia Bowerley (d. 1916).

Opposite
Goblin on a swing,
Charles Folkard (1878-1963).

Left
Goblins Tempting a Girl with their Fruit,
1939, Arthur Rackham.

Brownies, hobgoblins and goblins

> *"Though the goblins cuffed and caught her,*
> *Coaxed and fought her,*
> *Bullied and besought her,*
> *Scratched her, pinched her black as ink,*
> *Kicked and knocked her,*
> *Mauled and mocked her,*
> *Lizzie uttered not a word;*
> *Would not open lip from lip*
> *Lest they cram a mouthful in."*
> *Goblin Market*, Christina Rossetti (1830-1894).

Other European countries also have their domestic spirits that willingly make their presence known on the long nights of the winter solstice. Brownies for instance (or hobgoblins meaning the goblin by the hob beside the hearth) are domestic spirits that help to keep the house in order and carry out menial domestic chores. This is how Colin de Plancy describes them in the *Dictionnaire infernal*: "domestic imps that hide away in the most secluded parts of the house, beneath piles of wood. Their masters feed them on delicacies in exchange for the stolen corn that they bring from neighboring lofts." In English-speaking countries hobgoblins are such familiar figures that they are even known by name. There is Lazy Lawrence, guardian spirit of the orchard, Awd Goggie (from the East Riding of Yorkshire) that frightens children away from gooseberries, Melch Dick, the wood demon that protects unripe nuts from children and Kilmoulis, an ugly brownie that haunts the mills of Lowland Scotland.

Stevenson's brownies

In 1888 the Scottish novelist Robert Louis Stevenson, author of *Treasure Island* and *The Strange Case of Dr Jekyll and Mr. Hyde* published an article in the January edition of Scriber's Magazine expressing his gratitude towards the good brownies. His words suggest that he regarded these amiable creatures, friends of people of letters, almost as his alter egos:

"Who are the Little People? They are near connections of the dreamer's, beyond doubt; they share in his financial worries and have an eye to the bank-book; they share plainly in his training; they have plainly learned like him to build the scheme of a considerate story and to arrange emotion in progressive order; only I think they have more talent; and one thing is beyond doubt, they can tell him a story piece by piece, like a serial, and keep him all the while in ignorance of where they aim. Who are they, then? And who is the dreamer?

Well, as regards the dreamer, I can answer that, for he is no less a person than myself, [...] And for the Little People, what shall I say they are but just my Brownies, God bless them! Who do one-half my work for me while I am fast asleep, and in all human likelihood, do the rest for me as well, when I am wide awake and fondly suppose I do it for myself. [...] so that, by that account, the whole of my published fiction should be the single-handed product of some Brownie, some Familiar, some unseen collaborator, whom I keep locked in a back garret, while I get all the praise and he but a share (which I cannot prevent him getting) of the pudding."

Brownies

Unlike their European counterparts, brownies in the British Isles (Scotland, Ireland, Cornwall, on the west coast of England, the Orkneys, the Shetlands and the Channel Islands) are usually terribly lazy although well respected by local people. They are about a foot and a half to three feet tall, with a monkey-like appearance due to the thick brown fur that covers them from head to toe, revealing only their eyes of such piercing blue that once seen they are never forgotten. Brownies hate the cold and rarely stir from their favorite spot, curled up sound asleep by the hearth. Sometimes they amuse themselves by swinging on special "brownie swings" made from horseshoes hung on the walls.

These placid imps live off cream, honey cakes, black bread and bitter beer. They have a horror of knives, so never use one when preparing their supper. Never serve them directly or they might be so offended that they move away forever. Simply leave the food in a corner, as if by chance, where the brownies will pretend to find it, as if by chance, and relish it all the more.

One of their more important tasks is to deal with swarms of bees. If a swarm suddenly descends upon an English courtyard, the owner will ring a bell or beat a saucepan, shouting "Brownie, brownie!" at the top of his voice and the good brownies will rush out and chase the bees away.

Some of the most celebrated brownies are the famous Maggie Moulach, Hairy Meg, and her husband Brownie Clod, so-called because of his unpleasant habit of throwing clods of earth at passers-by for a joke. Both Meg and her husband were reputedly attached to the Grants of Tulllochgorum, from Strathspey in Scotland. Maggie Moulach would serve at table, floating through the air with whatever dish was requested before delicately landing on the table. She would also whisper words of advice into her master's ear when he was playing chess, telling him which pieces to move so as to win the game.

Left
Illustration by George Cruishank
(1792-1878) in *The Forbes Magazine*.

Below
Wag and the Wa, family of brownies.
"Today I'll bake; tomorrow I'll brew.
Then I'll fetch the queen's new child.
It is good that no one knows
Rumpelstiltskin is my name."
Rumpelstiltskin, The Brothers Grimm
(Jacob Grimm 1785-1863;
Wilhelm Grimm 1786-1859).

Right
Etching by F.C. Harrison
for *Marigold Mary*, 1910.

Opposite
Cluricauns, illustration 1873.

Brownies are also the guardians of brewers who in days gone by would offer them copious amounts of beer before starting to brew. In exchange, the brownies made sure that the ale produced had a bouquet and a bitterness second to none. But these practices with their pagan overtones were frowned upon by the Christian faith, as explained here by Walter Scott: "A young man in the Orkneys used to brew, and sometimes read upon his Bible; to whom an old woman in the house said, that Brownie was displeased with that book he read upon, which, if he continued to do, they would get no more service of Brownie; but he, being better instructed from that book, which was Brownie's eyesore and the object of his wrath, when he brewed, would not suffer any sacrifice to be given to Brownie; whereupon the first and second brewings were spoilt, and for no use; for though the malt liquid wrought well, yet in a little time it left off working, and grew cold; but of the third broust, or brewing, he had ale very good, though he would not give any sacrifice to Brownie, with whom afterwards they were no more troubled."

Leprechauns and cluricauns

Below
Irish leprechauns, engraving
by George Denham.
"Little Cowboy, what have you heard,
Up on the lonely rath's green mound?
Only the plaintive yellow bird
Sighing in sultry fields around,
Chary, chary, chary, chee-ee! –
Only the grasshopper and the bee? –
'Tip-tap, rip-rap,
Tick-a-tack-too!
Scarlet leather sewn together,
This will make a shoe.
Left, right, pull it tight;
Summer days are warm;
Underground in winter,
Laughing at the storm!'
Lay your ear close to the hill.
Do you not catch the tiny clamour,
Busy click of elfin hammer,
Voice of leprecaun singing shrill
As he merrily plies his trade?"
The Fairy Shoemaker, *William Allingham.*

Other celebrated hobgoblins that also do duty as domestic spirits are the Irish leprechauns, miniature cobblers in three-cornered hats whose little hammers may be heard tapping away in the thickets towards the end of winter. For reasons that no one quite understands, leprechauns generally resole a single shoe, never the pair. It is the leprechauns that invented hockey, by the way. They are also gifted violinists and there is nothing they like more than a good Irish whiskey and a pinch of snuff.

Then there are the cluricauns, wild old men in red caps, leather aprons, blue stockings and high-heeled shoes with silver buckles. They live in the hollow hills of Ireland minting forged coins and anyone catching a cluricaun can force it to give up its gold in exchange for its freedom. But beware, the cunning midget has no end of tricks up its sleeve to duck out of its obligations. Cluricauns are also said to be rather too fond of a drink and to raid the spirits in wine cellars. The Irish however are happy to overlook such minor misdemeanors because they are forever in the cluricans' debt: long ago, it was they who taught the inhabitants of the Emerald Isle the fabulous secret of whiskey.

Peer Gynt and the troll

Peer Gynt written by Norwegian author Henrik Ibsen in 1876 and set to music by Edward Grieg in 1876, is a dramatic poem about a whimsical character called Peer, a liar and a braggart whose excesses eventually prove the death of his mother, Aase. Peer is incapable of distinguishing between illusion and reality. One moment he is emperor of the world, the next he is weaving a fantastic tale about taking a ride through the clouds on a runaway reindeer. One day, he meets a pretty young girl called Solveig who spurns his attentions because he has had too much to drink. To revenge himself, Peer kidnaps his former fiancée Ingrid on her wedding day. He carries her off into the mountains where he shames her, then abandons her and takes off into the forest like a coward. It is at this point that he is smitten by the charms of the Lady in Green, daughter of Brose, king of the trolls, and follows her to the troll kingdom. Trolls are grotesque, malevolent creatures that reign over the fjords and mountains of Nordic regions and spend their time playing nasty tricks on men.

If Peer wishes to marry the Lady in Green he too must turn into a troll by adopting their crude, whimsical behavior. The troll king explains that trolls do not live by the same rules as men "In the mortal world, people say 'Man, know thyself but in the troll world we say 'Troll, be sufficient unto thyself.' Give me your word that from now on you will live and act by our motto." It is then that Peer Gynt realizes that he has spent his entire life pleasing himself and that all this time while he thought he was a man, he had actually lived like a troll. So he has no hesitation in giving the king his word. But then the king explains that Peer Gynt must also become as ugly as the trolls by growing a monstrous pig's tail and gouging out one of his eyes. When Peer refuses the troll children set upon him with their claws and teeth. In desperation, Peer calls on his mother for help and suddenly all the church bells start ringing. The trolls run away shrieking and Peer returns to the valley below where Solveig awaits.

Left
Illustration by Arthur Rackham.

Above
Forest Troll, 1913, John Bauer (1882-1918).

THE TROLLS OF THE GREAT NORTH

"Snouk but and snouk ben,
I find the smell of an earthly man;
Be he living, or be he dead,
His heart this night shall season my bread."
Red Etin

The great Nordic winter is also a time for trolls, monstrous, misshapen creatures with furry bodies, tangled, matted hair and long snotty noses. These giants of Scandinavia are reputed to be so huge that their hair is indistinguishable from the pine trees, their foreheads from the rocks and their beards from thorny thickets. Trolls are stupid, bloodthirsty creatures that can devour an entire herd of cattle with a single snap of their murderous jaws. They also have a highly developed sense of smell and can smell a human from a great distance. When they do, they fly into a blue rage shrieking, "I smell the blood of a Christian here."

Some trolls have multiple heads that must be severed with a single blow to stop them from growing back again. Their appetite is such that they can devour an entire ox in one bite. They are hardly discreet however and signal their arrival with a revolting chorus of snorts, grunts, hawks, sneezes, burps, farts and other equally nauseating sounds.

There is only one sure way to avoid being eaten by a troll and that is to ask the giant a series of riddles and puzzles. You see, strange as it may seem for such dim-witted spirits, trolls are crazy about brain-teasers and other problems. But since they are of very limited intelligence it takes them hours to find the answer, leaving the victim ample time to escape or simply wait till morning when the troll is forced to retreat. If it has not returned to its secret lair before sunrise, it will turn into a mountain which at the end of winter will blossom with the first spring faeries. And so the magical cycle will start all over again ....

Dragons

These fierce, fabulous monsters are the most powerful of all the animals ever imagined by medieval bestiaries. They are depicted as gigantic serpents with scaly bodies that can resist the sharpest weapons, one or more pairs of legs ending in clawed talons, batwings and thrashing, forked tails. There are black dragons, yellow dragons, white dragons (of Germanic origin) and red dragons from Wales that are reputed to be the most dangerous. Some have multiple heads with crowns of horns. Their chiseled jaws feature poisonous fangs and their noxious breath ignites on contact with the air. Dragons are in fact the animal versions of fire-eaters, capable of breathing out huge balls of fire that will ravage towns and forests in a flash. But even before they are burned, hapless creatures caught in the dragon's path are suffocated by its scorching breath.

All natural disasters are the fault of dragons. They dip their tails in rivers causing them to break their banks, pollute the waters where they bathe, scorch and burn the harvests and devour livestock. They also spread epidemics and bring misery and famine upon the land. In ancient times, young virgins would be sacrificed to these horrible beasts to appease their rampaging fury. Sometimes all of the town's virgins could be sacrificed in this way, as happened in the 3rd century AD in the town of Silene in Rome's African province of Libya. Finally it was the turn of the king's daughter to be immolated for the terrible creature, but in the nick of time she was rescued from the dragon's clutches by a valiant knight named George who died a martyr in 303 AD. Since then, Saint George slaying the dragon has symbolized the Christian struggle between good and evil, and in the 14th century St. George was established as patron saint of England.

Dragons hibernate deep inside their gloomy caves for years and even centuries, apparently sound asleep. But their stillness is deceiving because in fact they remain awake at all times – given their absence of eyelids, they could hardly do otherwise. Since time began, their uncanny ability to do without sleep has singled them out as the natural guardians of the treasures that lie buried in the depths of the Earth. These riches are reserved for courageous heroes such as Siegfried who dare to do battle with the fire-eating beast, driving their trusty blade right through its heart which is the only vulnerable part of a dragon's armor-plated body. The valiant dragon slayer must avoid being sprayed with the monster's bubbling blood, but by moistening his lips with a single drop he will instantly acquire the gift of bird language. Henceforth he will be able to understand everything the birds say which, as everyone knows, is often prophetic and always truthful.

Left
Illustration by Walter Crane.

Right
Les Beaux Contes (Nos Loisirs collection),
early 20th-century illustration.

The Night of Miracles

Christmas Night is sometimes known as the Night of Miracles. It is the night when animals are said to talk and all you need do is listen to hear their predictions. On Christmas Night, the trees turn green and blossom with flowers and fruits descended from Heaven. On the first stroke of midnight, buried treasures briefly come out of hiding then disappear again with the final stroke. Dragons awake from their year-long slumbers and dance by the light of the moon with silvery, silver-blooded unicorns. Christmas Night is steeped in folklore throughout the Celtic countries and especially on the Brittany Peninsula in France, between the English Channel and the Bay of Biscay. The people here believe that the Ankou, a sinister figure dressed in black and carrying a scythe like the Grim Reaper, enters churches during midnight mass and runs its bony fingers lightly over those who will be dead within the year.

To conclude our journey into the Kingdom of Faerie, let us now look at a selection of Christmas myths and legends from the ancient land of Brittany.

Doubting Thomas

There was once a skeptical old peasant who refused to believe in the miracles that happen on Christmas night, especially that animals can suddenly talk. So one Christmas he decided to see for himself and leaving his family at midnight mass he went to hide at the back of the stable to spy on his animals. When the bell rang for the Elevation, he saw his oxen kneel down and pray. At the end of their devotions they started to talk and to the peasant's astonishment he could understand every word. "The year will start badly," sighed one of the oxen. "We have an unpleasant task ahead." "Why is that?" asked the other. "We've finished the plowing, gathered in the crops and brought in enough wood to last all winter." "Yes," replied the first, "but we will have to pull a heavy cof-

Veille de Noël en Berry,
in *L'Illustration,* 1852.

fin all the way to the cemetery because our master, an unbeliever, is going to die this very morning." At these words our wretched peasant shrieked with horror and dropped dead on the stable floor — which is where his family found him when they returned from midnight mass. Since then, although animals have continued to talk on Holy Night, people have thought it best not to eavesdrop.

Galloping imps, errant stones and thieving witches

In Lower Brittany, people say that on the *Noz Petquent* ("Night of Miracles") legions of korrigans, poulpiquets, teus and korils emerge from their underground lairs to chase across the silvery strand and the reedy, windswept moors. Springs and wells resound to the song of nighttime washing women, water spirits and wood faeries.

It is the hour when dolmens half-open revealing their hidden treasures, cromlechs dance the roundel at the top of treeless mountains and teetering stones teeter. At the first stroke of midnight, the standing stones of Carnac quit their neat ranks to gallop like raging bulls towards Saint-Colomban Cove or the River Etel. Once there they plunge their stony muzzles into the water and gulp it down, knowing that when the clock finishes striking they must return to their places and remain motionless until the following Christmas. On the same night and at the same time, the menhir of La Houssaye goes to drink at a nearby spring. This is the only moment when it leaves its treasures unguarded and at the mercy of thieves. But woe betide anyone foolish enough to explore the hole left by the stone's departure for on the twelfth stroke of midnight it will return to resume its position, crushing the misguided intruder.

In Upper Brittany, people say that while the clock strikes the twelve strokes of midnight the Jugon standing stone goes to drink at the river Arguenon, and the Mont-Beleux stone is carried off by a blackbird.

On that night, witches in nightshirts walk naked through the woods, slipping their right hand under their left to pick a magical golden herb called Witches Grass that has the power to stop errant stones in their tracks and force them to relinquish their riches. Without the grass's protection the witches would be crushed to death before they could relieve the stones of their treasures. And even if they did manage to escape with their booty without being flattened, their ill-gotten gains would turn into dead leaves, lumps of coal and seashells.

Virgin power

The most fabulous of all the places in Lower Brittany where white faeries and tiny dus gather on the Night of Miracles is the Lew-Drez or "Place of the Strand" overlooking the great blue rock of Roc'Hél-Glas (or Roc Hellas) near the village of Saint-Michel-en-Grève.

On the stroke of midnight, an immense cavern opens up in the sand at high tide revealing treasures far beyond those ever possessed by any king: heaps of gold, gems, jewelry and the finest fabrics. In the deepest recesses of the cave lies the most precious object of all, a magical goblet that renders the bearer omnipotent. However desirable, this enchanted goblet has never been removed, being guarded not by a fierce, fire-eating dragon or mighty warriors but innocent maidens of such entrancing beauty that anyone contemplating them forgets all about the goblet and the time. On the twelfth stroke of midnight, the walls of the cave close in and anyone inside remains trapped forever. In living memory, nobody has ever returned to tell the tale.

The story of Jean Skouarn

In Ploumiliau, in Finistère at the extreme end of Brittany, there was once a brave young fellow by the name of Jean Skouarn who was told by a beggar that on Christmas Night the waves parted to reveal a magnificent castle where a beautiful princess was held prisoner. Anyone wishing to rescue the maiden and seize the castle's treasures had to cross all of its rooms between the first and the last stroke of midnight without stopping for a single moment. In the last room was a magic wand that rendered the bearer omnipotent. If however the mission ended in failure, the would-be hero would turn into stone.

Jean Skouarn decided to try his luck. One by one, he crossed all of the rooms without stopping to explore their mysterious contents. In the first room he glimpsed priceless treasures. In the second were dragons and fierce animals that threatened to attack him. In the third were languid young girls that tried to seduce him. In the fourth were the petrified figures of his predecessors. Finally he reached the last room containing the magic wand which he seized just as the clock struck the twelfth stroke of midnight. Thus did the valiant Jean Skouarn free the princess and inherit all of the treasures in the palace. Shortly afterwards he and the princess were married and our noble hero used some of his fortune to build a chapel where people still go and pray to this day.

The sunken city of Ys

On the same night in the Bay of the Trépassés (Bay of the Deceased), the waves part to reveal the sunken city of Ys that was forever swallowed up by the sea as punishment for the sins of its inhabitants. On that night, Saint Corentin descends to celebrate midnight mass in the brightly-lit cathedral. As the service draws to a close, the saint falls silent, turns towards the faithful and waits. If a single courageous mortal were to dive into the water, enter the sunken cathedral and pronounce the word "Amen," the city of Ys would emerge from the watery depths into the sunlight.

But should that day ever come, they say that Paris will sink to a watery grave and France will be looking for a new capital.

Left and preceding page
The nocturnal dance of elves and imps.

Right
L'engloutissement de la ville d'Ys,
engraving by Cipori, 1885.

Faery Index

Photographic credits

© AKG: p 79 (Kreismuseum, Heinsberg), 84-85 (Schack Galerie, Munich) 110, 113, 116, 126-127, 128 B, 131, 146 H, 146 B, 152, 154.

© AKG/Coll. Archiv fÜr Kunst & Geschichte, Berlin,: pp 102, 150, 153.

© HACHETTE ARCHIVES: pp 39 (© Arthur Rackham), 173.

© NANCY MUNICIPAL LIBRARY: pp 18, 21.

© ISABELLE MASSET PRIVATE COLLECTION: p 157.

© MUSÉE DE BRETAGNE COLLECTION: pp 176-177.

© FÉLIX LORIOUX, ADAGP PARIS 2002: pp 71 and 108, 109, 161.

© G. DAGLI ORTI: p 78 (Richard Wagner Museum, Bayreuth), pp 179, 180.

© KHARBINE TAPABOR: pp 49 (Coll. Grob), 31, 96, 97 H, 112 (Coll. Jonas), 14, 38, 46,73, 74 H, 74 B, 75, 76 M, 76 B, 77, 86 H, 94 H, 97 B, 101 B (Adagp, Paris 2002), 103, 119, 129, 130, 137, 143, 147, 148, 149, 151, 158, 160, 161, 174, 175, 178.

© KHARBINE TAPABOR/ARTHUR RACKHAM: 82 H, 115, 170.

© MARY EVANS PICTURE LIBRARY: pp 24, 34, 64, 68, 86 B, 87, 91, 111 H, 114, 167, 168 B, 169.

© MARY EVANS PICTURE LIBRARY/ARTHUR RACKHAM COLL.: pp 23, 37, 120, 165.

© MUSÉE DÉPARTEMENTAL BRETON, QUIMPER: pp 107 H, 107 B.

© OLIVIER GRUNEWALD: pp 32-33, 54-55,138-139.

© PHILIP PLISSON / PÊCHEUR D'IMAGES: p 132-133.

© ROGER-VIOLLET: pp 159, 181.

© STÜDEL MUSEUM, FRANKFURT: p 30.

© THE BRIDGEMAN ART LIBRARY: 16 (Bonhams, London), 22 (Walker Art Gallery, Liverpool, Merseyside), 36, 65 H (Christie's Images), 44 (British Library, London), 45 (Fitzwilliam Museum, University of Cambridge), 56-57 (Oldham Art Gallery, Lancashire), 58 (University of Liverpool Art Gallery), 66-67 (Christopher Wood Gallery, London), 69 (Harris Museum, Preston, Lancashire), 80-81 (The de Morgan Foundation, London), 82 B (Musée des Beaux-Arts, Quimper), 92-93 (Coll. of The Royal Theatre), 94 B (Museo Prado, Madrid), 98-99 (Julian Hartnoll, London), 100 (Musée des Arts Décoratifs, Paris/Peter Willi), 106 (Musée de Notre Dame, Strasbourg), 111 B, 117, 121, 122-123, 124 (The International Fine Art Auction), 125 (York City Art Gallery, North Yorkshire), 140-141 (Whitford & Hughes, London), 145 (Kinnaird/ F. Gerald Private Collection), 156 (The Gavin Graham Gallery, London), 166 (the Forbes Magazine Coll., N. Y., 168 H © Archives Charmet/Bibliothèque des Arts Décoratifs, Paris).

© THE BRIDGEMAN ART LIBRARY / ANTHONY CRANE COLL.: pp 142 H, 142 B.

© THE BRIDGEMAN ART LIBRARY/CHRIS BEETLE, LONDON: pp 17, 20, 35, 104-105, 164.

© THE BRIDGEMAN ART LIBRARY/PRIVATE COLLECTION: pp 12-13, 48, 62-63, 65, 72, 101 H, 162-163.

© THE BRIDGEMAN ART LIBRARY/NATIONAL MUSEUM, STOCKHOLM: pp 171, 172.

© THE BRIDGEMAN ART LIBRARY/ROY MILES FINE PAINTING: pp 42, 83.

© THE BRIDGEMAN ART LIBRARY/THE MAAS GALLERY, LONDON: pp 15, 16 H, 19, 23, 26-27, 29, 40-41, 50-51, 59, 61, 70, 128 H.

© THE BRIDGEMAN ART LIBRARY/VICTORIA & ALBERT MUSEUM, LONDON: pp 28, 47, 60, 95, 144.

Acknowledgements

My thanks to all the men and women whose elfin looks,
impish wit and faery words encouraged me to explore the shortcuts
to the faerie kingdom. With special thanks to Catherine,
alias Ange Catoue (Catoue Angel); Élodie, alias Mac-Loreen;
Pierre, alias Petrus Barbygère; Claude, alias Le Meneur de Loups
(Leader of The Wolf Pack); Philippe, alias Mouffette; Catherine,
alias Melmiriel; Damien, alias Le Buveur de Bière (The Beer Drinker);
not forgetting my faithful brownies, diligent workers in the realms of fancy;
and the fragrant good faery at the Bibliothèque Nationale for generously
placing her exceptional knowledge at my disposal.

Edouard Brasey

The publisher wishes to thank all those who helped to produce
this book, in particular Aldona Kucharska at Hachette Archives
and also Stéphanie Mastronicola for her many services.

Editor: Brigitte Leblanc
Creative Director: Sabine Houplain
Picture Research: Muriel Jeancard
Design and Layout: Amanda Mouseler
Proofreading: Catherine Lucchesi and Myriam Blanc

This book first published in France by Editions du Chene a division of Hachette-Livre.
This edition first published 2003 by Hachette IllustratedUK,
Octopus Publishing Group, 2/4 Heron Quays, London E14 4JP
Translation joint copyright Octopus Publishing Group

English translation by Florence Brutton
Printed in Singapore Tien Wah Press

ISBN 1-84430-041-2